Beading Vintage-Style Jewelry

EASY PROJECTS WITH
Elegant Heirloom Appeal

Marty Stevens-Heebner
& Christine Calla

A LARK/CHAPELLE BOOK

A Division of Sterling Publishing Co., Inc.
New York

Editor:
Kathy Sheldon

Art Director:
Susan McBride

Cover Designer:
Cindy LaBreacht

Assistant Editor:
Julie Hale

Associate Art Director:
Shannon Yokeley

Art Production Assistant:
Jeff Hamilton

Editorial Assistance:
Delores Gosnell
Mark Bloom
Cassie Moore

Illustrator:
Orrin Lundgren

Photographer:
Keith Wright

A Lark/Chapelle Book

Chapelle, Ltd., Inc.
P.O. Box 9255, Ogden, UT 84409
(801) 621-2777 • (801) 621-2788 Fax
e-mail: chapelle@chapelleltd.com
Web site: www.chapelleltd.com

Library of Congress Cataloging-in-Publication Data

Stevens-Heebner, Marty, 1961-
Beading vintage-style jewelry : easy projects with elegant heirloom appeal
/ Marty Stevens-Heebner and Christine Calla. -- 1st ed.
    p. cm.
Includes index.
ISBN 1-60059-070-5 (hardcover)
1. Beadwork. 2. Jewelry making. I. Calla, Christine, 1962- II. Title.
TT860.S755 2007
745.58'2--dc22

                                2006034628

10 9 8 7 6 5 4 3 2 1

First Edition

Published by Lark Books, A Division of
Sterling Publishing Co., Inc.
387 Park Avenue South, New York, N.Y. 10016

Distributed in Canada by Sterling Publishing,
c/o Canadian Manda Group, 165 Dufferin Street
Toronto, Ontario, Canada M6K 3H6

Distributed in the United Kingdom by GMC Distribution Services,
Castle Place, 166 High Street, Lewes, East Sussex, England BN7 1XU

Distributed in Australia by Capricorn Link (Australia) Pty Ltd.,
P.O. Box 704, Windsor, NSW 2756 Australia

If you have questions or comments about this book, please contact:
Lark Books
67 Broadway
Asheville, NC 28801
(828) 253-0467

Manufactured in China

ISBN 13: 978-1-60059-070-2
ISBN 10: 1-60059-070-5

For information about custom editions, special sales, premium and corporate
purchases, please contact Sterling Special Sales Department at 800-805-5489 or
specialsales@sterlingpub.com.

Contents

Introduction

Vintage jewelry—the term evokes visions of rich colors and classic designs. The timeless romanticism of heirloom jewelry is something jewelry lovers of every generation treasure, and beaded designs hold special appeal. Stroll through any antique store or museum jewelry collection and you'll see beaded necklaces, earrings, and bracelets that look fresh and fashionable to the modern eye. Artisans have used gemstones in their beaded jewelry for centuries to create a dance of color that includes cobalt blues, peridot greens, ruby reds, and more.

But what do you do if your vintage jewelry collection is limited to your grandmother's pearl necklace and earrings? Make your own, of course. With this book and a few tools and supplies, you can bead your own vintage-style jewelry—exquisite brooches, bracelets, earrings, and chokers that have the elegance of family heirlooms. And because you'll be the one stringing the beads, you can feel free to experiment with color, texture, and pattern. You can even customize each piece so that the jewelry you create complements your own taste, wardrobe, and sparkling personality.

We've organized the 48 pieces featured in this book into four categories: classic, elegant, romantic, and dramatic. Take a moment to skim the pages and you'll be amazed to discover that, though these elegant designs were inspired by the past, they remain very fashion forward. Not only are these necklaces and earrings remarkable for their elegance, they're also surprisingly versatile. Our lavish Lassoed Pearls necklace is perfect for a day at the office or an evening out. For a dose of vibrant color, try our French Follies Crystal Collar, a dramatic emerald green choker that can dress up a simple T-shirt and jeans as well as wow a cocktail party crowd.

Because many of our projects were inspired by designs from earlier eras, we invite you to think of this book as a trip back in time. As you look at our projects, you'll probably find that some of the jewelry seems familiar. That's because you may have seen similar pieces in old paintings and family photos. We've included Asian-inspired designs that date to the 1100s, delicate pearl earrings and chokers that evoke 19th-century England, and even pieces reminiscent of the swinging sixties.

Some of the pieces may seem intricate, but you'll be surprised at how simple they are to make. Even if you've never strung a bead or looped a piece of wire before, you'll be surprised by how easily you can complete any of our winsome designs. Our Basics section features information on supplies and techniques along with instructions and illustrations to familiarize you with the beading process, and advice on how to construct rebuilt pieces from thrift store finds. Make your way further into the book, and you'll see that each of the projects contains detailed step-by-step instructions to guide you through that particular piece.

The hardest part of making the pieces in these pages will be deciding where to begin. Should you start in the 1920s with our shimmering Flapper Necklace, or journey back to the Victorian era and make our classic Cameo Pin? The choice is yours. As you move from one project to the next—and travel from one epoch to another—you'll be creating your own collection of elegant heirloom jewelry you'll wear and treasure for years to come.

Vintage Jewelry *Basics*

Crafting chokers, brooches, and bracelets that have a quality of timeless elegance is easier than you think. In this chapter we'll get you familiar with the materials and tools you'll need to make vintage-style jewelry, and we'll show you how making this jewelry is essentially a matter of learning a few basic techniques you'll then repeat in various combinations. Let's look first at the materials and tools you'll be using.

Materials

The secret to achieving vintage style when making your own beaded jewelry is using the right materials. Picking the appropriate beads, threading materials, and findings is one of the most important parts of the creative process—luckily, it's also the most fun.

Beads

As you'll discover when you walk through the doors of a bead shop, an almost overwhelming variety of beads is available. The ones used in our vintage designs fall into three categories—crystal, pearl, and gemstone. Within each category, many variations exist. **Crystal beads**, for example, come in several different shapes, including cube, round, and bicone, as well as in innumerable color choices.

The letters AB, often used to describe crystal beads, refer to a special coating that's put on the surface of the crystal to add extra dimension and sparkle. The coating is usually of a pale blue or yellow hue. AB actually stands for "aurora borealis," the radiant lights that occasionally brighten the night sky in the northern latitudes.

If you think **pearls** are simply an accessory your grandmother wore, round and white, pretty but a bit too proper, think again. Pearls now come in a surprising variety of shapes and colors, and they're central to many of the pieces in this book. We used freshwater pearls in many of our designs, because they're affordable and easy to find. You can stick to the standard white or, if the piece you're working on dates back to a particular era, you can experiment with colors that were popular during that period.

Gemstones also come in a wide variety of types—garnets, amethysts, and peridots, to name a few. Gemstones come in different grades, as well. A grade A amethyst is deep violet in hue with no discoloration, while a B or C grade amethyst will be substantially paler and may contain streaks or spots.

When you're ready to start shopping for beads, find a supplier who's reliable and who stocks genuine, high-quality pieces. If you live in or near a major city, be on the lookout for bead shows. These craft events always offer a wonderful assortment of beads and beading materials.

Figure 1

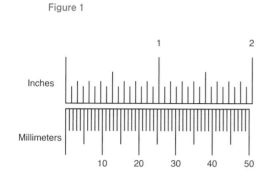

Figure 2

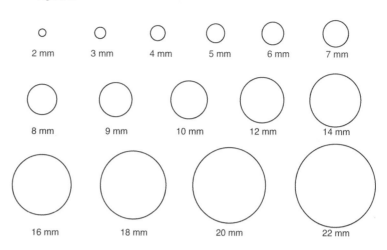

2 mm	3 mm	4 mm	5 mm	6 mm	7 mm
8 mm	9 mm	10 mm	12 mm	14 mm
16 mm	18 mm	20 mm	22 mm

BEAD SIZES

Regardless of their shape or type, beads are measured in millimeters, not inches (see figure 1). The millimeter measurement refers to the diameter of the bead, so that you know how much space it will occupy when it's strung (see figure 2). There are a couple of exceptions to this rule. **Drop beads**—the kind that have holes through the top—are measured in millimeters according to their length. **Seed beads**—the kind that look like tiny kernels—are sized according to number. The higher the number, the tinier the seed bead. Size 6 seed beads are the most typical type. You may see them listed in catalogues as 6/0 or 6°. They're also known as "E" beads.

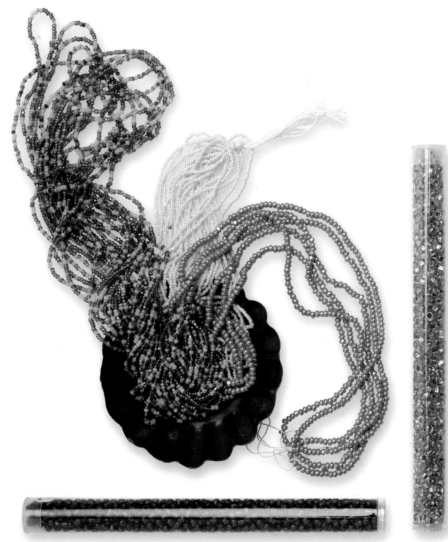

Threading Materials

There are three basic kinds of stringing material: tigertail wire, nylon line, and beading thread. Each has a different level of flexibility and strength, factors you should consider when planning your project.

Tigertail wire is a thin, pliable cable composed of woven wire strands. It comes in various diameters and strengths and can be used in just about any kind of beading project. The smaller the diameter (i.e., the lower the number), the thinner the cable. Thin cable tends to be very flexible, while thicker cable is stronger and better suited for heavy beads and gemstones. Experiment with different diameters of wire (.012, .018, and .024, for example) to see what works best for you. One of the benefits of working with tigertail wire is that it's stiff enough to go through a bead on its own. You won't need a beading needle if you're using this kind of wire.

Metal wire. Whether it's sterling silver or gold-filled, metal wire adds a unique shimmer to any piece of jewelry. Metal wire is measured in gauges: the higher the number, the thinner the wire. For example, 16-gauge wire is substantially thicker than 28-gauge wire, which is quite thin. (Note that tigertail wire is measured in the opposite way.) Metal wire also comes in different densities: dead soft (the most malleable), half-hard, and full hard (the hardest to bend). Try experimenting with different gauges and densities to see what works best for you.

KEY TO WIRE GAUGES

The projects in this book were made using wire manufactured in the United States, whose standards for wire diameters differ from those in the British system. AWG is the acronym for American, or Brown & Sharpe, wire gauge sizes and their equivalent rounded metric measurements. SWG is the acronym for the British Standard, or Imperial, system in the UK. Refer to the chart below if you use SWG wire. Only part of the full range of wire gauges that are available from jewelry suppliers is included here.

AWG IN.	AWG MM	GAUGE	SWG IN.	SWG MM
0.204	5.18	4	0.232	5.89
0.182	4.62	5	0.212	5.38
0.162	4.12	6	0.192	4.88
0.144	3.66	7	0.176	4.47
0.129	3.28	8	0.160	4.06
0.114	2.90	9	0.144	3.66
0.102	2.59	10	0.128	3.25
0.091	2.31	11	0.116	2.95
0.081	2.06	12	0.104	2.64
0.072	1.83	13	0.092	2.34
0.064	1.63	14	0.080	2.03
0.057	1.45	15	0.072	1.83
0.051	1.30	16	0.064	1.63
0.045	1.14	17	0.056	1.42
0.040	1.02	18	0.048	1.22
0.036	0.914	19	0.040	1.02
0.032	0.813	20	0.036	0.914
0.029	0.737	21	0.032	0.813
0.025	0.635	22	0.028	0.711
0.023	0.584	23	0.024	0.610
0.020	0.508	24	0.022	0.559
0.018	0.457	25	0.020	0.508
0.016	0.406	26	0.018	0.457

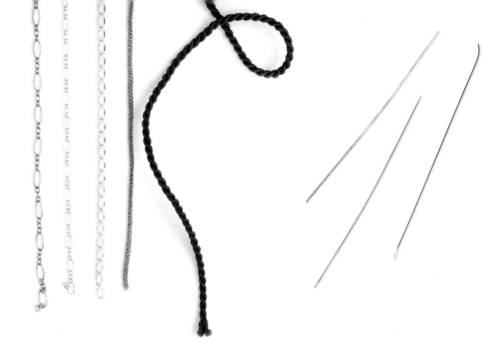

Nylon line is an excellent material for beading because it's clear and durable. Make sure you buy nylon line that's specifically made for jewelry design. Don't use clear fishing line—it stretches easily and can break unexpectedly. Nylon line designated for jewelry making, however, is strong and produces a clean look, particularly with translucent beads.

Decorative cords. Unlike other types of stringing material, decorative cords are meant to be shown off and are included as part of the jewelry design. We use romantic elements like organza ribbon and velvet in many of our designs. Chain is also featured, in gold or silver.

Nylon or silk beading thread comes in different colors and thicknesses. Nylon thread is easy to work with and doesn't fray, although it may stretch over time. When choosing a thread, make sure you pick one that's thin enough to easily fit through the smallest bead you'll be stringing. Keep in mind that—

depending on the type of project you're doing—you may need to run the thread through the bead a few times. Whenever possible, choose thread in a color that matches the beads you'll be using. Otherwise, select a color that's lighter than the beads in your design.

Beading needles are essential if you're going to use beading thread. Thread is simply so slack that a needle is required for sliding it through a bead. Some brands of thread come with a short needle already woven onto one end. Big-eyed needles are wonderful to work with—and not just because they're easy to thread.

They're pliable and can handle multiple strands of thread at the same time. The needle's large eye closes up as soon as it's pushed through a bead, and you can easily reopen it with a pin or awl for rethreading.

When working with tiny seed beads or creating intricate stitches, more conventional needles are required. For these types of projects, beading needles that resemble standard sewing "sharps" and are numbered according to size—10, 13, 15, and so on—will do the trick. Remember that the larger the number of the needle, the thinner it will be.

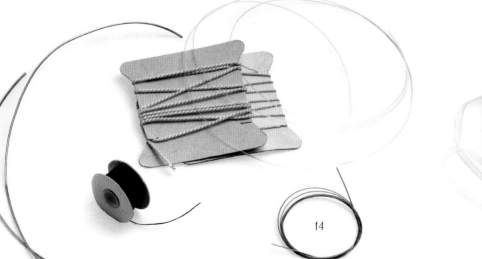

Findings

Findings are the metal components that hold jewelry together. These include earring wires, jump rings, clasps, and more elaborate elements like chandelier and silver filigree findings.

Clasps are the means by which you open and close a bracelet or necklace. There are countless styles of clasps, so choose one that enhances your vintage design. A clasp can be composed of one or two parts and will contain a loop so that you can attach it to your beading string.

Crimp beads resemble small metal beads or tubes, and they can be used to connect a clasp to a necklace or bracelet (see page 000). A crimp bead will have a large opening relative to its size. When pinched or "crimped" around stringing material, the bead holds the material firmly in place. Crimp beads are chiefly used with tigertail and other types of flexible beading wire that don't knot well.

Bead tips are excellent for finishing bracelets or necklaces strung on bead thread. They hold and hide the knots at either end of a piece of jewelry, and possess a loop you can attach to a clasp. Clam shell bead tips are widely used because they have two bead cups that, when clamped together, hide knots completely. Some jewelry makers attach a bead tip before they begin stringing their beads. However, if you're still experimenting with your bead design, don't add the bead tips until after you've finished stringing your beads, so that you can adjust the design more easily.

Head pins and **eye pins** are straight bits of wire available in various lengths and different metals. They're usually sold in packets of a dozen or more. A single head pin has a flat "stopper" at one end, which makes the pin look like a long, skinny nail. This stopper prevents beads from sliding off. Eye pins have stoppers in

To prevent tangles from occurring, slide the thread along some beeswax before you begin to string the beads.

To ease the frustration of threading, pick the largest needle (it will have the largest eye) that will fit through the smallest bead hole in your design.

Bear in mind that seed beads are numbered the same way beading needles are numbered. Therefore, a size 11 needle should fit through a size 11 seed bead. Remember that if your design calls for you to make more than one pass through a bead, you should use thinner thread and a smaller needle.

the form of round loops. After adding beads to a head pin or eye pin, use round-nose pliers to form a loop in the straight end of the pin (see page 19). You can use this loop to attach the pin to another component.

Earring findings provide a multitude of ways for designing earrings. Ear wires are available in many forms, including French, Spanish, and kidney wires, as well as simple posts with small loops for attaching beads. Clip-on and screw-on findings are also available for non-pierced earrings.

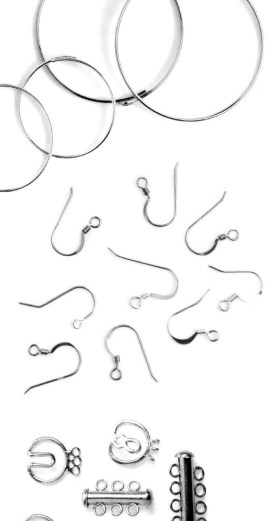

If you're a beginner, it's a good idea to choose an earring finding with a loop that can be opened and closed. You can easily add your completed beadwork to this type of finding. However, if you've purchased closed-loop findings, don't worry—just make sure you take this factor into account as you're beading.

Jump rings are simple wire circles of various sizes that are split along their circumference. They're ideal for connecting a pendant to a necklace or a clasp to a bracelet. **Split rings** are similar to jump rings. They're composed of double loops of wire and resemble tiny key rings. Split rings are more difficult to open and harder to work with than jump rings. But a split ring won't be pulled open by the weight of a heavy necklace the way a jump ring sometimes is.

Spacers are decorative metal findings that come in two types. The first are small, disk-shaped filler beads that add subtle shimmer to a design. The other kind of spacer—an ornate metal bar containing two to five holes—is used with multiple-strand jewelry. By threading one strand each through one of the holes, you can keep your strands orderly and avoid tangling. End spacers have two or more loops on one side and a single loop on the other side that you attach to a clasp.

Other findings run the gamut from pin backs and barrettes to bead caps that can be used to add a bit of shimmer to your jewelry. These pieces are available in catalogs, at your local craft and bead stores, and online. Investigate what's out there and don't be afraid to experiment. You never know where your creativity will lead.

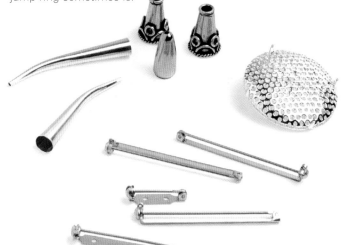

Glue

Glue is a vital component of jewelry making. It prevents knots from coming untied and keeps beads secure. **Bead glue** or **cement**—sold in most craft shops—is typically used to seal knots. The glue comes in a small tube that has a needle-like applicator. Instead of using the applicator, which can be messy, put a few drops of glue on a needle or straight pin and apply the glue to your knots, making sure you don't spread the glue to the surrounding beads. If no glue is available, **clear nail polish** will suffice for securing knots.

A **hot-glue gun** and **glue sticks** will come in handy for tasks such as attaching a large stone to a pin back. You should also have an **industrial strength adhesive** or **sealant** on hand. Most bead stores carry large tubes of this type of glue—it's very handy for securing beads or wire to other objects, like picture frames or mirrors.

basic tool kit:

—●◆●—

To complete the projects in this book, you'll need the following tools:

- Craft scissors
- Wire cutters
- Pliers

Tools

You may have seen the larger versions of these tools at the hardware store. Jewelry-making tools are smaller and made for doing delicate work. They're available at most craft shops.

Craft scissors

Used for everything from cutting lengths of wire to trimming strands of ribbon. They are indispensible.

Wire cutters

Wire cutters come in a variety of styles. **Diagonal cutters** allow you to trim hard-to-access areas. A sturdy set of **end cutters** should serve you well for the projects in this book.

Pliers

Round-nose pliers are used to make loops and curves. Their jaws are tapered and cylindrical, so you can wrap wire around them.

Needle-nose pliers have a flat inner surface and jaws that taper to a pointed end. Because of their spear-like tip, needle-nose pliers can slip into tight spaces. Needle-nosed pliers are also known as chain-nose pliers or snipe-nose pliers. Just be sure to use a pair with a smooth edge on the inside of the jaws—pliers with a serrated inside edge can damage wire.

Shaping Tools

Other handy items for beading include a **tapered mandrel** and **dowels** of various sizes. A mandrel is a rod used for coiling wire—you can

wrap wire around it to form loops, or use it to make jump rings and other circular forms. Dowels—made from wood or steel—are also good for fashioning precise circles and rings.

Other Tools

A **beading board** can be helpful when you're putting your designs together. They're inexpensive and easy to find. A typical board has inch markers, so you'll know how long your string of beads will be, as well as small, built-in compartments that let you organize your beads and keep them separated as you work. Most boards have separate grooves for each strand of a multiple-strand necklace.

Tweezers are also handy for picking up small beads.

Basic Techniques

Once you get a few standard techniques under your belt, you'll find that what seems like a complicated piece of jewelry is often just a combination of quite simple forms. We'll look first at the common techniques used to create wire jewelry.

Wire Loops and Links

Loops and links hold together many of these projects, so becoming proficient at wire bending is a must. Don't despair if your results look less than spectacular at first—making attractive loops and links really is just a matter of practice.

JUMP RING

Figure 3

The only thing you need to learn to use these simple wire circles is how to open and close them correctly. Don't open a jump ring by pulling the ends apart to make the circle larger—this will distort the shape of the ring and weaken the wire. Instead, use two pairs of pliers to grip the ring on either side of the split. Now gently pull one side away from you and the other side toward you (see figure 3). Add your bead, charm, or clasp, and close the ring by reversing the motion.

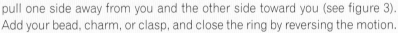
Figure 4

BASIC LOOP

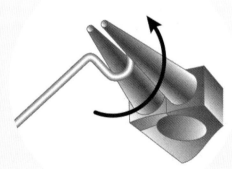
Figure 5

To begin making a basic loop, first use round-nose pliers to make a 90° bend about ½ inch from one end of the wire (see figure 4). (Exactly where you bend the wire will depend on the size of the loop you wish to make.) With the long end of the wire pointing toward the floor and the short, bent end pointing toward you, grasp the short end with the round-nose pliers, holding the pliers so the back of your hand faces you. Rotate the pliers up and away from you to create half a loop (see figure 5). Be careful not to distort the 90° angle in the wire. Adjust the pliers' position, and then continue bending the wire into the complete loop (figure 6). Make sure one of the pliers' tips is snug and stationary inside the loop as you bend. Stop when the loop closes against the 90° bend.

Figure 6

Figure 7

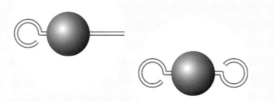

BASIC LOOP LINK

To make a basic loop link, simply make one basic loop, slide a bead or beads onto the straight section of wire, and then form another basic loop that faces the opposite direction at the other end of the wire (see figure 7).

WRAPPED LOOP

To make a wrapped loop, follow the instructions to form the basic loop, but use a longer length of wire for the bent section. When you've made the loop, slide the lower jaw of the pliers into it, and then use your other hand to wrap the extra wire around the loop's base several times (see figure 8).

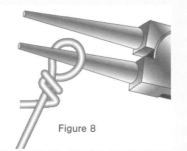

Figure 8

WRAPPED LOOP LINK

To make a wrapped loop link, just make a wrapped loop on one end of the wire, slide on a bead or beads, and then make another wrapped loop that faces the opposite direction on the other end of the wire (see figure 9).

Figure 9

Wire Stringing Basics

To make a simple, single-strand bracelet or necklace using tigertail wire, do the following:

1 Use the craft scissors to cut a piece of tigertail wire that's the intended length of your necklace plus a minimum of 4 inches.

2 String the beads for your bracelet or necklace onto the wire.

3 String a crimp bead onto each end of the piece. Thread a clasp onto one end, then wind the wire around and back through the crimp bead and the first couple of beads (see figure 10). Pull the end of the wire until the crimp bead butts up against the clasp. Now crimp the bead using the needle-nose or crimping pliers, and trim away any excess wire with the scissors.

4 Repeat step 3 with the other end, but this time use a jump ring or split ring instead of the clasp. Make sure to pull the wire until it's tight, so that no gaps remain between the beads.

Figure 10

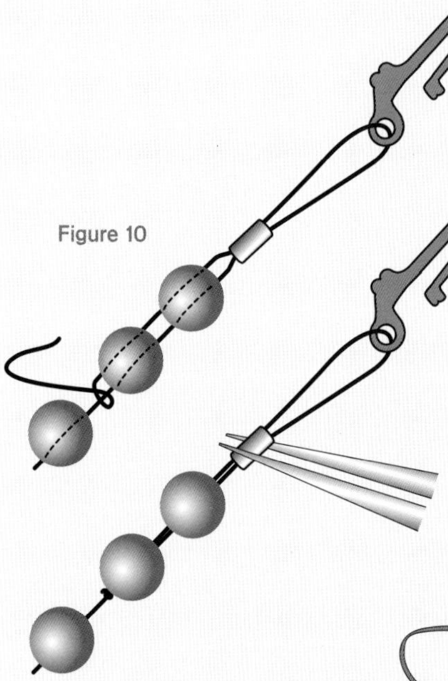

tuck it into the cup of the bead tip, then knot it again. Add a bit of bead cement to the knots, then trim the thread close to the knots. Attach the bead tip's hook to the end of your clasp and close the hook with a pair of needle-nose pliers.

Figure 11

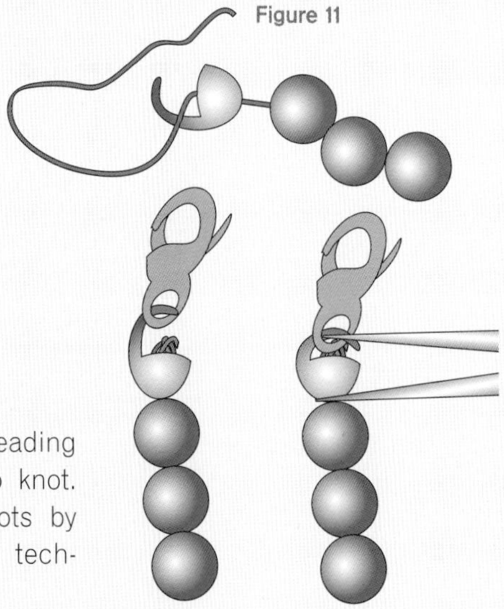

through a closed jump ring. Wrap the thread around the ring twice, and then slide the needle back through several beads. Knot the thread (see figure 12). Slide the needle back through a few more beads and knot the thread again. Add a dab of bead glue to the knots and trim away any excess thread. Carefully open the jump ring and attach the clasp to it to complete the piece.

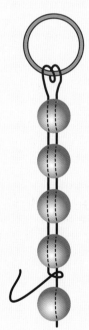

Stringing Beads with Thread

Unlike most bead wire, beading threads are usually easy to knot. You can then hide the knots by using various findings or techniques.

USING A BEAD TIP

To use a simple bead tip, slide your needle and thread through the bead tip, making sure that the hook on the bead tip faces outward, toward the end of your bracelet or necklace (see figure 11). Knot the thread,

USING A JUMP RING TO FINISH A THREADED PIECE

If you like, you can finish a piece of jewelry using a jump ring and beading thread. At one end of your string of beads, slip your threaded needle

Figure 12

Rebuilt Vintage Jewelry

T ake a look in your jewelry box. Got an old costume necklace that's broken? How about a contemporary one with a design that just doesn't work? Those pieces you never wear but can't quite bear to discard are actually undiscovered treasures waiting for you to come to their rescue, to work your magic and recycle them into something spectacular. All it takes are a few findings, some extra beads, and your own sense of style to make as many as four new pieces from just one necklace.

To get started reworking a piece, gather a variety of tools, findings, and extra beads so that you can experiment. Sometimes you won't know what you should make from a piece until you take it apart. This can be the hardest part: we're so used to living in fear of a necklace breaking that to break it intentionally feels wrong. But take a deep breath and snip away—though make sure you do so over a bowl or towel that will catch the beads.

Your creations can be as simple or as intricate as you like. For easy earrings, slide a large bead onto a headpin, make a loop in the end with the round-nose pliers, and attach an earring wire. String the beads onto tigertail wire and attach a clasp to make a necklace. Do the same to make a bracelet, or make an even simpler one using beading elastic.

We transformed this vintage necklace into a bracelet, earrings, and a pin.

If you've got a hot-glue gun, use it to make an elegant brooch or scarf pin—just glue a pin back to a large bead or stone. But first, be sure to examine the pendant from a variety of angles. With the pin pictured here, we decided that placing the pendant on its side made for a much more intriguing piece. Don't be afraid to experiment. The bigger polka dot beads in the original necklace just cried out "ponytail holder" to us. We made ours with thin sewing elastic, because it does a better job of gripping hair than regular beading elastic.

You never know what those old, neglected pieces at the bottom of your jewelry box might become. The only limit is your own imagination.

Lurking within this groovy necklace was a ponytail holder, bracelet, and earrings, just waiting to be made.

Classic
◆◇◆

Some jewelry designs have a resonance that simply transcends time. The luster of pearls entices just as much now as it did during the Renaissance. And images, whether carved on cameos or captured in photos encased in silver, have always had a special allure. The classic designs in these pages are enduring favorites you'll treasure for years to come.

25

Tiers of Pearls Set

This timeless set pairs lustrous freshwater pearls

with brilliant red crystal beads.

To make the necklace:

What You Need

Basic tool kit (page 17)

Tigertail wire

47 red crystal bicone beads,
4 mm diameter

172 white freshwater pearls,
5 mm diameter

2 end spacers with 3 holes each

6 crimp beads

Hook clasp

2 jump rings

Silver chain for necklace
extender (optional)

Headpin for necklace extender
(optional)

What You Do

1 Cut three 20-inch pieces of the tigertail wire. Begin the first strand of the necklace by stringing one of the red crystal beads onto a strand of the wire, then string the following pearl pattern onto the strand, separating each group of pearls with a crystal bead: 4 pearls, 5 pearls, 3 pearls, 5 pearls, 3 pearls, 5 pearls, 3 pearls, 4 pearls. Repeat this pattern in reverse (4-3-5-3-5-3-5-4), then finish the strand with a crystal bead. This strand should be approximately 16 inches long.

2 To make the second strand of the necklace, string one of the crystal beads onto a piece of the wire, then string the pearls onto the wire in the following pattern, separating each cluster of pearls with a crystal bead: 5-5-7-3-4-3-4-3-4-3-7-5-5. Finish the strand with a crystal bead. This strand should be approximately 15 inches long.

3 To make the third strand of the necklace, string a crystal bead onto the final 20-inch piece of tigertail wire, then add pearls in the following pattern, separating each cluster with a crystal bead: 3-4-5-4-3-3-3-3-3-3-4-5-4-3. Add a crystal bead at the end. This strand should be about 14 inches long.

4 Lay the three strands next to each other on a table, so that the shortest strand is at the top and the longest strand is at the bottom. Place end spacers at both ends of each strand, then slide a crimp bead onto both ends of each strand.

5 Thread one end of the 14-inch strand through the top loop of the end spacer, then back through the crimp bead and the first crystal bead. Pull the end of the wire until the crimp bead butts up against the end loop, then crimp the bead using the needle-nose pliers and trim away any excess wire with the scissors. Do the same to the other end of the strand, making sure the wire is pulled tightly enough so that no gaps remain between the beads.

6 Repeat step 5 with the two other strands of the necklace, attaching the 15-inch strand to the middle loop of the end spacer and the 16-inch strand to the last loop.

7 Open the jump ring attached to the clasp, slip this ring through the single loop at the top of one of the end spacers, then close it using the needle-nose pliers. Add a jump ring to the other end spacer in the same manner.

8 If desired, make a necklace extender by cutting a 1½-inch piece from the silver chain with the wire cutters. Open the jump ring from step 7 with the needle-nose pliers and slip it through one end of the chain, then through the single loop atop the other end spacer. Close the jump ring.

9 To complete the extender, slide a crystal bead onto the headpin. Grasp the end with the round-nose pliers, and wrap the wire around one prong of the pliers to form a small loop. Slide this loop through the loose end of the silver chain. Wrap any remaining wire around the pin between the bottom of the loop and the top of the bead using the needle-nose pliers.

To make the bracelet:

What You Need

Basic tool kit (page 17)

Tigertail wire

87 freshwater pearls, 4 mm diameter

8 spacer bars, each with 3 holes

26 red crystal bicone beads, 4 mm diameter

6 crimp beads

Clasp

Jump ring

Silver chain for bracelet extender (optional)

Headpin for bracelet extender (optional)

What You Do

1 Cut three 10-inch lengths of the tigertail wire.

2 Slide one of the pearls onto a piece of the wire, then thread the wire through the top hole of one of the spacer bars. Add four pearls and one of the crystal beads to the strand, then thread the wire through the top hole of the second spacer bar. String a crystal bead and four pearls onto the strand and add a spacer bar. Repeat this pattern two more times, making sure to thread the wire through the top hole of the spacer bar each time.

3 Thread four pearls and a crystal bead onto the strand, followed by the sixth spacer bar and another crystal bead to complete the pattern. This strand should be approximately 6 inches long.

4 Repeat steps 2 and 3 with another piece of the tigertail wire, but thread the strand through the hole on the opposite side of the spacer bars, making sure to leave the middle hole empty for now.

5 Begin the third strand of the bracelet by sliding a crystal bead onto it, then thread the wire through the center hole of the first spacer bar.

6 String a crystal bead onto the strand followed by four pearls and a spacer bar, again threading the wire through the center hole. Now add four pearls, a crystal bead, and the third spacer bar. Repeat this pattern two more times.

7 For the last segment of the bracelet, string a crystal bead and four pearls onto the strand, slip the wire through the final spacer bar, then add a pearl to finish the strand. Lay the three strands down next to each other on a flat surface and slide one of the crimp beads onto each end of the pieces of wire.

8 Take one end of the first strand and thread the wire through the jump ring attached to the clasp. Then thread it back through the crimp bead and the first crystal bead. Pull the end of the wire until the crimp bead butts up against the jump ring, then crimp the bead and trim away any excess wire.

9 Repeat step 8 with the opposite end of the strand, using the jump ring and making sure the wire is pulled tightly enough so that no gaps remain between the beads. Then repeat steps 8 and 9 with the two other strands to finish the bracelet.

To make the earrings:

What You Need

Basic tool kit (page 17)

10 headpins

12 red crystal bicone beads, 4 mm diameter

18 white freshwater pearls, 5 mm diameter

24-gauge silver wire

Silver chain, 2 inches long

12 white freshwater pearls, 3 mm diameter

2 earring hooks

tip —••—

You can use either a jump ring or an end spacer to join the ends of the bracelet together. Either design works—it's just a matter of personal taste.

What You Do

1 Slide a crystal bead onto one of the headpins, then add one of the 5 mm pearls. With the round-nose pliers, grasp the headpin ½ inch from the end and make a small loop. Using the needle-nose pliers, wrap the remaining wire around the pin between the bottom of the loop and the top of the bead, then trim any excess wire. Repeat this procedure with a second headpin.

2 Repeat step 1 with two more headpins, this time threading two pearls onto the pin instead of one. Then repeat this process with a fifth headpin, adding three pearls this time.

3 Cut a 2-inch length of the 24-gauge wire, grasp the wire ½ inch from one end with the round-nose pliers, and make a small loop. Then slide this loop through one end of the chain. Wrap the remaining wire two to three times beneath the bottom of the loop with the needle-nose pliers, and trim any extra wire.

4 Slide one of the 3 mm pearls onto the wire. Thread one of the headpins from step 1 onto the wire, then slip another 3 mm pearl onto the strand, followed by one of the 2-pearl headpins. Add another 3 mm pearl and the 3-pearl headpin to the strand. Then alternate the smaller pearls with the remaining 2-pearl headpin and 1-pearl headpin, respectively.

5 Grip the wire ½ inch from the end with the round-nose pliers, make a small loop, then slide the loop through the other end of the silver chain. Wrap the remaining wire between the bottom of the loop and the last pearl, using the needle-nose pliers. Trim any extra wire, then bend the wire slightly to create a gentle curve in the pearls.

6 Cut a 1-inch piece of the 24-gauge wire, then grasp the wire ½ inch from the end with the round-nose pliers and make a small loop. Slide this loop through the center link of the silver chain, then wrap the remaining wire two to three times beneath the bottom of the loop using the needle-nose pliers. Trim any extra wire.

7 Slide a crystal bead onto the wire and form another loop in the opposite end, then attach the end to the loop of one of the earring hooks. Repeat the process to make the second earring.

10 If desired, make a bracelet extender by cutting a 1-inch piece of the silver chain with the wire cutters. Use the needle-nose pliers to open the jump ring from step 9, then slip one end of the chain onto the jump ring and close the ring.

11 To complete the extender, slide a crystal bead onto the headpin. Grasp the end with the round-nose pliers, and wrap the wire around one prong of the pliers to form a small loop. Slide this loop through the remaining end of the silver chain. Wrap any remaining wire around the pin between the bottom of the loop and the top of the bead using the needle-nose pliers.

Ladder-of-Beads Ribbon Choker

This versatile piece is easy to make using a simple length of ribbon and a ladder of pearls. Wear it as a necklace or a headband by tying the ribbon at the nape of the neck, or wrap it around the wrist for a dramatic effect.

What You Need

Basic tool kit (page 17)

2 strands of freshwater pearls, each 16 inches long, 4 mm diameter

Clear, ultra-fine nylon beading line, 2 yards

Crimp bead

1 yard of organza ribbon, ¼ inch wide, with ends cut on the diagonal

Fray retardant

tip —◆◆◆—

This beading pattern is called the ladder stitch.

What You Do

1   Thread eight freshwater pearls onto the nylon line, positioning them in the center. Separate three pearls from the others on one side, then take one end of the nylon line and thread it through these three pearls. Pull the nylon line until it's tight, making sure you keep the pearls centered on the strand so that they form a small oval.

2   Add one pearl to each side of the nylon line and position it so that it adjoins the pearls from step 1. Slide three more pearls onto one side of the nylon line, then thread the other end of the nylon line through these three pearls and pull the line tightly to form another oval (see figure 1).

Figure 1

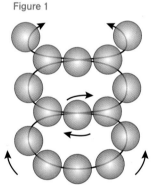

3   Repeat step 2 until one inch of nylon remains at each end (35 to 40 repetitions, or until no more pearls remain). The beaded area should measure 8 inches. Slide the crimp bead onto one end of the nylon line, then thread the opposite end of the line through it as well. Pull the line until it's tight, so that no gaps remain in between the beads, then crush the crimp bead and trim any excess nylon line.

4   Apply the fray retardant to each end of the organza ribbon. Let the ribbon dry according to manufacturer's instructions, then gently thread it in between the lines of pearls. Make sure that the ribbon emerging from each end is the same length. To wear this piece, simply tie the ends in a secure bow.

Copper Kernel Necklace and Earrings

Treasured during virtually every epoch in history, pearls have a timeless quality. This dainty set pairs copper-colored freshwater pearls with a delicate chain.

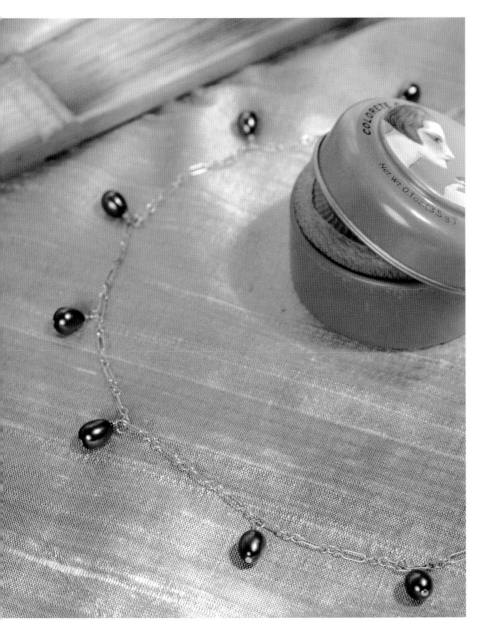

To make the necklace:
What You Need

Basic tool kit (page 17)

Chain

12 freshwater pearls, 5 x 4 mm

12 headpins

2 jump rings

Clasp

What You Do

1 Cut a 16-inch length of the chain. Thread one of the freshwater pearls onto a headpin, grasp the end of the headpin with the round-nose pliers, and form a loop by winding the wire around one of the prongs. Slide the loop through a chain link approximately 1¼ inches from the end, then wrap the remaining wire two to three times between the loop and the pearl. Trim any excess wire.

2 Repeat the first step 11 additional times, spacing each pearl approximately 1¼ inches from the last.

3 Open one of the jump rings, slide it through an end link in the chain, then close the ring. Open the other jump ring and slide it through the opposite end link and through the bottom loop of the clasp. Then close the ring.

To make the earrings:

What You Need

Basic tool kit (page 17)

6 freshwater pearls,
5 x 4 mm

6 headpins

2 pieces of chain,
each 1 inch long

2 earring wires

What You Do

1 Slide a freshwater pearl onto one of the headpins, then use the round-nose pliers to make a loop in the headpin just above the bead. Slip the headpin through one of the end links of the chain and wrap the remaining wire two to three times between the loop and the bead. Trim any excess wire.

2 Repeat step 1 to make two more beaded wires, then attach the wires to the same end link of the chain. Open the bottom loop of one of the earring wires, slip the other end link of the chain onto this loop, and close it. Repeat the process to make the matching earring.

Pearl Cluster Necklace and Earrings

Groups of freshwater pearls and blue seed beads give this set

an air of classic elegance.

To make the necklace:
What You Need

Basic tool kit (page 17)

Nylon beading thread, 72 inches

Beading needle

2 strands of seed beads in various shades of blue, each 16 inches long

80 round freshwater pearls, 4 x 3 mm

Chain, 2 inches long

2 jump rings, 8 mm

Headpin

Clasp

What You Do

1 Make a knot in the nylon beading thread about four inches from one end (this will keep the beads from sliding off the thread). Then string the opposite end of the thread through the beading needle and string 10 seed beads onto the thread, randomly mixing different shades of blue. Stitch through the beads a second time with the needle so that they form a loop. Add three more seed beads, a freshwater pearl, and another seed bead, making sure to slide the beads up against the beaded loop. Then stitch through the first two of these seed beads a second time.

2 Add a seed bead, a pearl, and another seed bead, then stitch through the same two beads a third time, and let this group settle next to the previous group of beads. Repeat this combination of beads until you've formed a cluster with five pearls around the center (see figure 1).

Figure 1

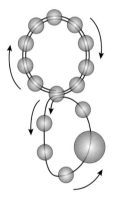 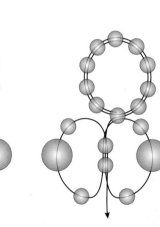

3 String 13 more seed beads onto the strand, followed by a pearl and another seed bead. Stitch through the 11th and 12th seed beads in this group a second time. Repeat step 2 to create a full cluster. Then repeat steps 2 and 3 fourteen more times.

4 Thread 10 seed beads onto the nylon thread, then stitch through the beads a second time so that they form a loop. Tie a double knot in the thread to secure the strand, and trim any excess thread.

5 Open one of the jump rings with the needle-nose pliers, and slide the ring through the first beaded loop and one of the end links of the piece of chain. Then close the jump ring.

6 Slide a pearl onto the headpin, and use the round-nose pliers to make a loop in the end of the pin. Then slide this loop through the remaining end link of the chain. Wrap the wire two to three times between the loop and the pearl, and trim any excess wire.

7 Repeat step 5 with the other jump ring and the opposite end of the strand, this time attaching the bottom loop of the clasp instead of the chain.

Oh, so faux!

The first known method of producing fake pearls comes from a book published in 1440. The volume contains a recipe for fake pearls that combines small shells, fish scales, powdered glass, egg white, and snail slime—yes, snail slime.

It wasn't until sometime in the 17th century that a Parisian rosary manufacturer named Francois Jaquin finally produced an acceptable method for making fake pearls. His patented technique included coating hollow, blown-glass balls with a varnish containing iridescent ground fish scales. The hollow balls were then filled with wax, which strengthened them. The result was so impressive that for the next 200 years, Paris was the place to find the best fake pearls.

To make the earrings:

What You Need

Basic tool kit (page 17)

Nylon beading thread, 12 inches

Beading needle

24 seed beads in various shades of blue

2 earring wires

10 round freshwater pearls, 4 x 3 mm

All-purpose glue or jewelry cement

What You Do

1 Make a knot in the piece of nylon beading thread approximately 4 inches from one end. String the opposite end of the thread through the beading needle, then string 10 seed beads onto the thread, randomly mixing different hues of blue.

2 Slip the nylon thread through the bottom loop of an earring wire, then stitch through the 10 seed beads a second time. Tie a knot at the end of the thread to secure the beads. String three seed beads, a freshwater pearl, and another seed bead onto the strand, then stitch through the first two beads from this step a second time.

3 Add a seed bead, a pearl, and another seed bead, then stitch through the same two beads, letting this group settle next to the previous one. Repeat this combination of beads until you've formed a cluster with five pearls around the center.

4 Tie the nylon thread and the 4-inch tail from step 1 together to secure the earring, then trim any excess thread. Apply a drop of all-purpose glue or jewelry cement to the knot, and let the earring dry according to the manufacturer's directions. Repeat the process to make the second earring.

Queen Victoria's Cameos: Choker and Pin

These matching cameo pieces will add a touch of class to your jewelry collection.

The pin is an easy-to-make variation on the traditional choker.

To make the choker:

What You Need

Basic tool kit (page 17)

Cameo, 40 x 30 mm

Bezel to hold the cameo

24-gauge wire

7 rectangular carnelian beads, 15 x 10 mm

144 freshwater pearls, 4 mm diameter

Clasp

Chain, 3 inches long

Headpin

What You Do

1 Lay the cameo inside the bezel and secure it by gently squeezing the top loop of the bezel with the nylon-jaw pliers. (Needle-nose pliers can also be used if the serrated edges are covered with masking tape to protect the bezel.)

2 Cut a 2½-inch piece of the 24-gauge wire. Grasp the wire ½ inch from the end with the round-nose pliers, make a loop by wrapping the wire around one of the prongs of the pliers, then slip it through the loop at the top of the bezel. Wrap the remaining wire two to three times around the base of the loop, and trim any excess. Slide a carnelian bead onto the wire, and make a loop in the opposite end approximately 8 mm in diameter. Wrap the wire two to three times between the loop and the bead, and trim any excess wire. Repeat this step to attach a second carnelian to the cameo.

3 Cut a 3½-inch piece of the 24-gauge wire, make a loop in one end with the pliers, and slip it through the large loop of one of the beaded wires from step 2. Wrap the wire as in step 2, then thread 12 freshwater pearls onto the wire. Repeat this step two more times so that you have a total of three wires with pearls attached.

4 Repeat step 2, this time hooking the first loop through the remaining end loops of the beaded wires from step 3. Then repeat step 3.

5 Repeat steps 3 and 4 on the other side of the necklace. Then repeat step 2 to attach an additional beaded wire to one end of the necklace, this time slipping the bottom of the clasp onto the second loop of the beaded wire.

6 Repeat step 2, this time slipping one of the end links of the piece of chain onto the second loop before wrapping it closed.

7 Slip a carnelian bead onto the headpin, make a loop in the end with the pliers, and thread it through the remaining end link of the chain. Wrap the wire two to three times between the loop and the bead, and trim any excess wire.

Tidbit

For centuries cameos were obtainable only by the well-to-do, but the Industrial Revolution changed that. By the mid-1800s, cameos made in English factories from glass or Wedgwood porcelain paste were widely available and very popular. Now it seems that each new generation of jewelry lovers is drawn to this emblem of the Victorian era. Fetch that cameo from your mother's jewelry box, and claim it as your own!

What You Need

All purpose glue or jewelry cement

Bezel

Cameo, 40 x 30 mm

16-inch strand of freshwater pearls, 2 mm diameter

Pin back

What You Do

1 Add a few drops of all-purpose glue or jewelry cement to the inner edge of the bezel, then lay the cameo inside the bezel. Gently squeeze the bezel's edge around the sides of the cameo with the nylon-jaw pliers to secure it. (Needle-nose pliers can also be used if the serrated edges are covered with masking tape to protect the bezel.) Let the piece dry.

2 Apply a thin line of all-purpose glue or jewelry cement around the sides of the bezel and the cameo. Then carefully wind the strand of freshwater pearls twice around the cameo and let the glue dry according to package the manufacturers instructions.

3 Apply the pin back to the cameo. If it's an adhesive back, simply peel off the protective strip and press it into place in the middle of the back of the pendant. Otherwise, apply a few drops of all-purpose glue or jewelry cement to the middle of the back of the cameo and attach the pin back.

Faces in Time Photo Bracelet

Nothing says vintage like an old-fashioned watch. This one-of-a-kind bracelet

lets you re-use treasured timepieces while showing off favorite photos.

What You Need

Basic tool kit (page 17)

Photographs

4 to 6 empty watch faces, depending on the size of the bracelet (A watch—or jewelry—repair person can remove the insides of the watch faces, so that only the frames remain. Keep the clear glass covers and set them aside.)

Tigertail wire

Ernite crystal bicone beads, 6 mm diameter

Crimp bead

Clasp

32-gauge wire

Ernite crystal bicone beads, 4 mm diameter

Freshwater pearls, 4 x 6 mm

What You Do

1 Trim the photos so that they fit inside the frames of the watch faces, then slip them into place. Press the clear glass into place over the top of each watch face to secure the photos inside.

2 Cut a 4-inch piece of the tigertail wire, thread it halfway around the first spring bar of one of the watch faces, then slide a 6 mm ernite crystal bicone bead, a crimp bead, and the clasp onto both ends of the wire. Wind both ends of the wire around the clasp and back through the crimp bead. Crush the crimp bead, and then trim any excess wire.

3 Cut a 4-inch piece of the 32-gauge wire, slide the wire halfway around the spring bar of the first watch face, and add a 4 mm ernite crystal bicone bead to both sides of the wire. Wrap the beaded wire tightly around the spring bar, then add another 4 mm bicone bead. Wrap the wire around the spring bar again, then twist the wire tightly at the back of the spring bar to secure it. Trim any excess wire. Repeat this step on the other side.

4 Cut a 4 ½-inch piece of the tigertail wire, and thread it through one of the holes on the side of the second watch face. String a freshwater pearl onto the wire and thread it through the other hole. Then string a 4 mm bicone bead onto either side of the wire. Add a 6 mm bicone bead and a crimp bead to both ends of the wire, then wrap the ends of the wire around the spring bar of the first watch face. Thread both ends of the wire back through the crimp bead, crush the crimp bead, and trim any excess wire.

5 Repeat step 4, but attach the wire to a spring bar from the third watch face. Repeat step 3, this time using two freshwater pearls and two 4 mm bicone beads. Repeat step 3, attaching the wire to the hidden spring bar of the fourth watch face.

6 Cut two 4-inch pieces of the 32-gauge wire. Coil one piece of wire tightly around the hidden spring bar on either side of the attached bicone bead. (These coils will prevent the beaded wire from lurching to one side.)

7 Repeat step 6 with the other spring bar. Then repeat step 2 to attach the fifth watch face, making sure to wind the tigertail wire between the coiled 32-gauge wires.

Art Deco Double Strand Necklace

Clean lines and a black-and-white color scheme make this necklace an Art Deco-inspired treasure. The striking pendant is made from black-banded agate.

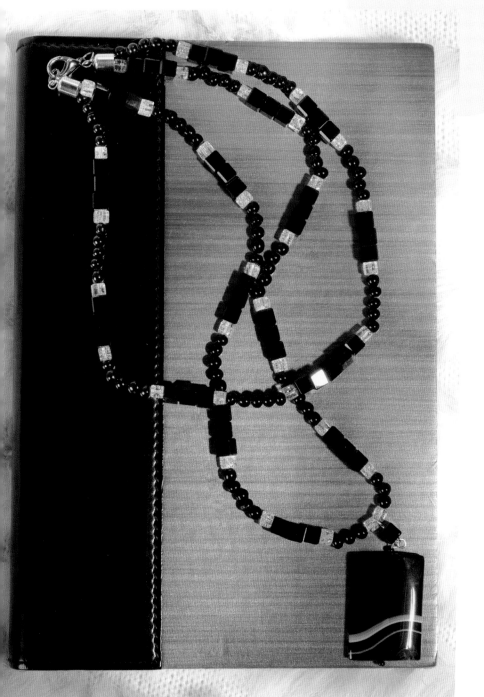

What You Need

Basic tool kit (page 17)

Tigertail wire

Black round beads, 4 mm

Cracked crystal quartz cube beads, 4 mm

Black cube beads, 6 mm

4 crimp beads

3 eyepins

2 black seed beads

Headpin (at least 2 inches long)

Black-banded agate pendant, 35 x 25 mm

2 end caps

Clasp

Jump ring

What You Do

1 Cut a 19-inch piece of the tigertail wire, and string beads onto the strand in the following order: 5 black round beads, 1 cracked crystal quartz cube bead, 3 black cube beads, and 1 cracked crystal quartz cube bead. Repeat this pattern twice, then repeat it again using five black cube beads instead of three.

2 Continuing with the same 19-inch strand of wire, repeat step 1 three more times, then add five black round beads to finish off the strand.

3 Slide a crimp bead onto both ends of the wire. Take one end of the strand and thread the tigertail wire through the loop of one of the eyepins. Now thread it back through the crimp bead and the first black round bead. Pull the end of the wire taut until the crimp bead butts up against the eyepin's loop. Now crimp the bead using the needle-nose pliers, and trim away any excess wire. Repeat with the opposite end of the strand, making sure the wire is pulled tightly enough so that no gaps remain between the beads.

4 Cut a 22-inch piece of the tigertail wire. String beads onto it in the following order: one cracked crystal quartz cube bead, three black cube beads, one cracked crystal quartz cube bead, and five black round beads.

5 Repeat step 4 four more times, but only add three black round beads to the last repetition. Then add one cracked crystal quartz cube bead.

6 String a black seed bead onto the headpin. Slide the pendant onto it, followed by a second black seed bead. Make a loop in the end of the headpin using the round-nose pliers, then slide this loop onto the loop of an eyepin, and secure it. Add one black cube bead to the eyepin and make a loop in the opposite end, then trim away any excess wire from the headpin and eyepin.

7 Thread the pendant onto the tigertail wire. Add one cracked crystal quartz cube bead, followed by three black round beads. Then repeat step 4 four additional times. Add one cracked crystal quartz cube bead, three black cube beads, and one cracked crystal quartz cube bead to finish out the strand.

8 Slide a crimp bead onto both ends of the wire. Take one end of the strand and thread the tigertail wire through the loop of the same eyepin from step 3. Then thread the wire back through the crimp bead and the first cracked crystal quartz bead. Pull the end of the wire until the crimp bead butts up against the eyepin's loop, and crimp the bead using the needle-nose pliers. Trim any excess wire.

Repeat this process with the opposite end of the strand, making sure the wire is pulled tight, so that no gaps remain between the beads. The two strands should now be connected by the eyepins.

9 Thread one of the eyepins through an end cap. Form a loop in the end using the round-nose pliers, and slide the clasp onto it, then close the loop securely using the needle-nose pliers, and trim away any excess wire. Repeat this step with the other eyepin, substituting the jump ring for the clasp.

Tidbit

The term "Art Deco" was coined during the Exposition Internationale des Arts Decoratifs et Industriels Modernes, which was held in Paris in 1925. Known for its bold, intense color combinations and for its cubist designs, the style itself officially spans the years 1925 to 1940.

Romantic

Light, love, and brilliance—
that's what romance is all
about. So it's no surprise
that flowers, lace and
sparkling jewels have
always warmed our hearts
and delighted the senses.
Wear any of the vintage
jewelry designs in this
chapter and you're sure to
draw many a glance,
especially if there's
candlelight.

Crystal Swing Earrings

Dangling, dazzling earrings have been a fashion staple in almost every age, from the Italian Renaissance to the swinging sixties. These crystal earrings are a contemporary take on an enduring classic.

What You Need

Basic tool kit (page 17)

2 red crystal beads, 15 x 12 mm

2 headpins

Chain, 2 inches

28-gauge wire, 8 inches

2 clear crystal beads, 8 x 5 mm

2 round filigree beads, 16 mm

2 earring wires

What You Do

1 Slide a red crystal bead onto one of the headpins, then use the round-nose pliers to make a loop in the end of the pin. Cut a 1-inch length of the chain, and slide the headpin's loop through an end link in the chain. Wrap the remaining wire two or three times between the loop and the bead, and trim any excess wire.

2 Cut a 2-inch piece of the 28-gauge wire, then use the round-nose pliers to grasp the wire approximately ½ inch from the end. Create a loop in the wire with the pliers, and slide this loop through the other end link in the chain. Then wrap the remaining wire end two to three times at the base of the loop, and trim any excess wire.

3 Slide one of the clear crystal beads onto the wire. Make a loop in the opposite end of the wire with the round-nose pliers, then thread the loop through an opening in one of the round filigree beads. Wrap the remaining wire two to three times between the loop and the last bead. Trim any excess wire.

4 Cut a 2-inch piece of the 28-gauge wire, and make a loop in one end of the wire using the round-nose pliers. Slip this loop through an opening in the filigree on the opposite side of the bead, then wrap the wire two to three times beneath this loop. Make a loop adjacent to the wire wrapping, and slide it through the bottom loop of an earring wire. Wrap the remaining wire two to three times next to or on top of the previous wire wrapping, then trim any excess wire. Repeat the process to make the other earring.

Radiant Rubies Hair Comb

What could be more romantic than a jewel-encrusted hair comb? Glittering with red crystal beads, this classic accessory is the epitome of vintage chic.

What You Need

Basic tool kit (page 17)

28-gauge wire, 24 inches

Hair comb

5 red Swarovski crystal 2-hole spacer beads, 15 mm

10 red crystal bicone beads, 4 mm

4 red Swarovski crystal 2-hole spacer beads, 12 mm

What You Do

1 Cut a 12-inch piece of the 28-gauge wire, and thread one end between the first two prongs of the hair comb. Use the needle-nose pliers to wind the wire around the base of the comb three times, making sure that at least ½ inch of the end of the wire remains free. Twist the remaining wire around the longer piece of wire two to three times to secure it.

2 Slide a 15 mm Swarovski crystal spacer bead onto the wire, and wrap the wire around the comb's base. Thread the wire through the bead and around the comb a second time, making sure to pull the wire until it's tight each time. Repeat this step until the entire base of the comb is covered with beads.

3 Wrap the remaining wire two to three times around the base of the comb at the other end, pulling the wire until it's tight each time. Thread the end of the wire between the wrapped wire and the base of the comb to secure it. Trim any excess wire.

4 To add the red bicone beads and the top row of 12 mm spacer beads, cut a 12-inch piece of the 28-gauge wire. Thread

one end of the wire behind the first spacer bead and between the first two prongs of the hair comb, then repeat the rest of step 1.

5 Thread a red bicone bead onto the wire, stopping ½ inch from the base. Fold the wire around the bicone bead and twist the bead onto the wire, then slide one of the 12 mm spacer beads onto the wire. Wrap the bead and the wire so that the spacer bead comes to rest between the second and third 15 mm spacer beads beneath it. Wind the wire once around the comb's base, then thread a red bicone bead onto the wire, twisting into the wire as before.

6 Repeat step 5 three more times to complete the top row, adding additional red crystal beads as desired. Repeat step 3 to finish out the hair comb.

Blue Rhapsody Necklace and Earrings

In this colorful set, blue bicone beads alternate with lengths of fine chain to create a look that's delicate yet festive.

What You Need

Basic tool kit (page 17)

24-gauge wire

2 jump rings

19 blue AB bicone crystal beads, 4 mm

Chain

17 clear AB bicone crystal beads, 4 mm

9 blue round crystal beads, 6 mm

Pendant (optional)

What You Do

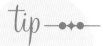

Add a bit of whimsy to your pendant! Slide a few colorful beads onto a headpin and make a loop at the end of the pin with the round-nose pliers. You can wrap this loop through the bail on your pendant and drape the beads, or hang the pendant by a bit of chain. Loop the headpins through a link or two from your chain, then use jump rings to attach it to the pendant.

1 Cut a 1½-inch piece of the 24-gauge wire with the wire cutters, then use the round-nosed pliers to grasp the wire approximately ½ inch from the end, and create a loop by wrapping the wire once around one of the prongs of the pliers. Slip this loop through a jump ring, then wrap the tail of the wire two to three times around the base of the loop. Slide one of the blue AB crystal bicone beads onto the wire, and form a loop with the opposite end of the wire.

2 Cut a 1½-inch length of the chain with the wire cutters, and slip the wire loop from step 1 through one of the end links. Then wrap the wire two to three times between the loop and the bead, and trim any excess wire.

3 Cut a 2-inch strand of the 24-gauge wire, and use the round-nosed pliers to create a loop in one end of the strand. Slip the wire through the opposite end link of the chain, then wrap the remaining wire two to three times around the base of the loop.

4 Slide one of the blue AB crystal bicone beads onto the wire, then add a clear AB crystal bicone bead, a blue round crystal bead, another clear bicone bead, and another blue bicone bead. Then form a loop in the opposite end of the wire with the pliers.

5 Repeat steps 2 through 4 seven additional times. Then cut a 1½-inch piece of chain with the wire cutters. Slip the wire loop from the last completed beaded wire through an end link of the chain, then wrap the wire two to three times between the loop and the bead. Trim any excess wire.

6 Repeat step 1, this time connecting the first loop of the wire to the remaining end link of the chain before beading it. If desired, slide a pendant onto the necklace. Then enclose the clasp in the second loop of the beaded wire, and wrap the remaining wire two to three times between the loop and the bead. Trim any excess wire.

51

What You Need

Basic tool kit (page 17)

Chain

4 blue round crystal beads, 6 mm

14 headpins

24-gauge wire

18 blue AB bicone crystal beads, 4 mm

2 jump rings

2 earring wires

12 clear AB bicone crystal beads, 4 mm

What You Do

1 Cut a 1-inch piece of the chain. Slide one of the 6 mm blue round crystal beads onto one of the headpins, then use the round-nose pliers to grasp the headpin approximately ½ inch from the end, and make a loop in the pin by wrapping the wire once around one of the prongs of the pliers. Slip this loop through one of the end links of the chain, then wrap the tail of the wire two to three times around the base of the loop. Trim away any excess wire.

2 Cut a 1-inch piece of the 24-gauge wire, and make a loop in one end of the strand with the round-nose pliers. Slip this loop through the other end link of the chain, then wrap the tail of the wire two to three times around the base of the loop, and trim away any excess wire. String a 4 mm blue AB bicone crystal bead onto the strand and form another loop in the opposite end of the wire with the pliers. Hook this loop through one of the jump rings, then wrap the wire two to three times between the loop and the bead, and trim any excess wire.

3 Cut two 1½-inch lengths of chain, then use the needle-nose pliers to open the jump ring and slip one end link from each piece of chain onto the jump ring, placing the links on either side of the beaded chain length from steps 1 and 2. Slide the open jump ring onto the loop at the bottom of one of the earring wires, then close and secure the jump ring.

4 Cut a 2-inch piece of the 24-gauge wire, then make a loop in one end with the round-nosed pliers. Slip this loop through the remaining end link of one of the chains from step 3, wrap the tail of the wire two to three times around the base of the loop, and trim away any excess wire.

5 Slide a 4 mm blue AB bicone crystal bead onto the wire, followed by a 4 mm clear AB bicone crystal bead, a 6 mm blue round crystal bead, another clear AB bicone bead, and a 4 mm blue AB bicone bead. Then form another loop in the opposite end of the wire with the pliers, and hook this loop through the end link of the other chain length from step 3 to form a triangle with a dangle in the middle. Wrap this wire two to three times between the loop and the bead, then trim away any excess wire.

6 Slide a 4 mm blue AB bicone bead onto one of the head-pins. Using the round-nose pliers, create a loop with the end and slip it through the center link of one of the chains on the side of the triangle. Wrap the tail of the wire two to three times around the base of the loop. Trim away any excess wire. Repeat on the opposite side.

7 Repeat step 6 four additional times, using clear AB bicone beads instead of blue, and attach the beads on either side of the blue beads from step 6. Repeat the process to make the second earring.

Sparkling Briolette Necklace

When it comes to vintage jewelry design, nothing can match the ageless elegance of briolette beads. In this sparkling strand, they're paired with **copper-colored seed beads**.

What You Need

Basic tool kit (page 17)

Tigertail wire, 21 inches

Seed beads

17 round beads, 6 mm diameter

16 briolette beads, 14 x 14 mm

2 crimp beads

Toggle clasp

What You Do

1 String 32 seed beads (2½ inches) onto the strand of tigertail wire. Add one of the round beads, another seed bead, then one of the briolette beads. Follow with another round bead, a seed bead, then a briolette bead.

2 Continue with the combination of seed bead, round bead, seed bead, and briolette bead, until all of the briolettes and round beads have been strung. Then add 32 seed beads.

3 String one of the crimp beads onto each end of the necklace. Thread the circular part of the toggle clasp onto one end, then wind the wire around and back through the crimp bead and the first seed bead or two. Pull the end of the wire until the crimp bead butts up against the toggle; then crimp the bead, and trim away any excess wire.

4 Repeat step 3 with the bar part of the toggle clasp on the opposite end of the strand. Make sure that the wire is pulled tightly enough so that no gaps remain between the beads.

tip

Gentle contrast plays an important part in the color scheme of this necklace. For an antique feel, stick to subtler hues of blue, brown, or red. For a more modern approach, try experimenting with magenta or metallic tones.

Tidbit:

A necklace belonging to Christine's grandmother inspired this design. Why not look at your mother's or grandmother's jewelry for ideas?

55

French Follies Crystal Collar and Bracelet

Dramatic and colorful, this charming crystal set was inspired by the Folies Bergère of Paris. Only the most vivid hues would do for the elaborate costumes worn by the showgirls there at the turn of the last century.

To make the collar:
What You Need

Basic tool kit (page 17)

Clear, ultra-fine nylon beading line

Beading needle (optional)

120 peridot green crystal bicone beads, 10 mm

All-purpose glue or jewelry cement

125 cobalt blue crystal bicone beads, 3 mm

24 medium blue crystal bicone beads, 6 mm

65 headpins, 2 inches long

24 medium green crystal bicone beads, 6 mm

10 jump rings, 8 mm

Chain

Clasp

What You Do

1 Cut a 4-yard piece of the nylon line and make a knot in one end, leaving a tail that is two inches long. (If desired, thread the opposite end through the beading needle.) Slide four of the peridot green crystal bicone beads onto the nylon line, then thread the nylon line back through the first three of these beads to form a circle.

2 Add three more peridot green crystal beads, then thread the nylon line back through the last bead from step 1 and the first two beads strung as part of this step (see figure 1). Repeat this step 24 more times. On the last set, thread the nylon line through all three of the added beads, then wind the nylon line inside and through the circle of beads two times and knot it tightly. Add a drop of all-purpose glue or jewelry cement to this knot and to the knot from step 1. Let the glue dry according to the manufacturer's directions.

3 Slide a cobalt blue crystal bicone bead and a medium blue crystal bicone bead onto one of the headpins. Thread this beaded headpin through the first peridot green bicone bead at the end of the strand. Using the round-nose pliers, grasp the headpin just above the peridot bead and make a loop in the end. Wrap the remaining wire two to three times between the loop and the peridot bead. Trim any excess wire (see figure 2).

4 Slide a cobalt blue crystal bicone bead onto another headpin, then add a medium green crystal bicone bead and two additional cobalt bicone beads. Make a loop in the end of the pin with the round-nose pliers, and slip it through the loop in the beaded headpin from step 3. Wrap the remaining wire two to three times between the loop and the top of the beaded wire from this step, then trim any excess wire.

5 Slip a cobalt blue crystal bicone bead onto another headpin, add a peridot green crystal bicone bead, and make loop in the end using the pliers. Slide this loop through the loop from the beaded headpin in step 4. Wrap the remaining wire two to three times between the loop and the top of the beaded wire from this step, then trim any excess wire.

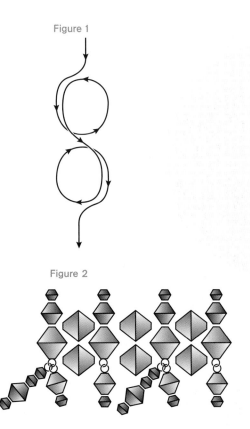

Figure 1

Figure 2

6 Repeat step 3, this time using a medium green bead instead of a medium blue crystal bicone bead. Then repeat step 4, substituting a medium blue bead for the medium green crystal bicone bead.

7 Repeat steps 3 through 6, alternating between medium green and medium blue beads, until the entire strand has been filled with beaded headpins.

8 Open one of the jump rings, then slip the ring through the beaded circle at one end of the strand. Close the ring and secure it, so that it rests on one side of the end peridot green bead. Add a second jump ring to the other side in the same fashion. Open a third jump ring and slip it through the first jump ring added, then hook a fourth jump ring through the third jump ring and the second jump ring added.

9 Cut a 3½-inch length from the chain and secure one of its end links to the fourth jump ring. Slide a cobalt blue crystal bicone bead and a peridot green crystal bicone bead onto a headpin, then make a loop in one end of the pin with the round-nose pliers, and slip it through the opposite end link. Wrap the wire two to three times between the loop and the peridot bead, and trim any excess wire.

10 Repeat steps 8 and 9 with the opposite end of the crystal bead strand, this time adding a clasp instead of a beaded headpin to the end via a jump ring.

To make the bracelet:

What You Need

Basic tool kit (page 17)

Beading elastic, 5 mm

Beading needle (optional)

50 peridot green crystal bicone beads, 10 mm

All-purpose glue or jewelry cement

120 cobalt blue crystal bicone beads, 3 mm

40 medium blue crystal bicone beads, 6 mm

80 headpins, 2 inches long

40 medium green crystal bicone beads, 6 mm

What You Do

1 Cut a 2-yard piece of the beading elastic and make a knot in one end, leaving a tail 2 inches long. (If desired, thread the opposite end through the beading needle.) Slide four of the peridot green crystal bicone beads onto the elastic, then thread the elastic back through the first three of these beads to form a circle.

2 Add three more peridot green crystal beads to the strand, then thread the elastic back through the last bead from step 1 and the first two beads strung as part of this step. Repeat this step 16 more times. On the last set, thread the elastic through all three added beads, then wind the elastic inside and through the circle of beads two times, and knot it tightly to secure it. Add a drop of all-purpose glue or jewelry cement to the knot and to the knot from step 1. Let the glue dry according to the manufacturer's instructions.

3 Slide a cobalt blue crystal bicone bead and a medium blue crystal bicone bead onto one of the headpins, then thread the headpin through the first peridot green bicone bead on the bracelet elastic. Use the round-nose pliers to grasp the headpin just above the peridot bead, and create a loop by wrapping the wire

once around one of the prongs of the pliers. Wrap the remaining wire two to three times between the loop and the peridot bead. Trim any excess wire.

4 Slide a cobalt blue crystal bicone bead onto another headpin, followed by a medium blue crystal bicone bead and two additional cobalt bicone beads. Make a loop in the end using the round-nose pliers, and slip it through the loop from the beaded headpin in step 3. Wrap the remaining wire two to three times between the loop and the top of this step's beaded wire, trimming any excess wire. Repeat this step two more times.

5 Repeat step 3, this time adding a medium green bead to the headpin instead of a medium blue crystal bicone bead. Thread the headpin through the peridot bead going in the opposite direction, then repeat step 4, substituting medium green beads for the medium blue crystal bicone beads each time.

6 Repeat steps 3 through 5, alternating between medium green and medium blue beads, until the entire bracelet has been filled with beaded headpins.

Blue Petal Shoe Clips

For a romantic look from head to toe, try these charming

shoe clips on for size.

What You Need

Basic tool kit (page 17)

22-gauge gold-filled wire

2 shank buttons, 16 x 13 mm

156 light blue frosted seed
beads, size 6/0

168 gold-colored seed beads,
size 11/0

Hot glue and hot-glue gun

2 clip-on earring backs

What You Do

1 Cut a 20-inch piece of 22-gauge wire. Slip ½ inch of the wire through the hole in one of the shank buttons, then secure the wire by twisting it two or three times with the needle-nose pliers and your fingertips. Trim any excess wire.

2 Gather 13 light blue frosted seed beads and 14 gold-colored seed beads. Slide a gold-colored bead onto the wire, then alternate between the light blue beads and the gold-colored beads until all the beads have been threaded onto the wire. Draw the beaded wire into a loop, and wrap the wire around the base two to three times. Repeat steps 1 and 2 five more times for a total of six beaded petals.

3 Thread the end of the wire through the buttonhole, twist the wire two or three times to secure it, and trim any excess wire. Then spread the beaded wires so the petals align evenly.

4 Apply a dollop of hot glue over the buttonhole, press one of the earring backs into the glue, and let the piece dry. Repeat the process to make the second clip.

Retro Marcasite Set

While it's undeniably retro and romantic, marcasite jewelry also has modern appeal. Here, marcasite findings are combined with smoky quartz and glistening marigold beads for a look that's as contemporary as it is stylish.

To make the necklace:

What You Need

Basic tool kit (page 17)

24-gauge wire

Marcasite finding

Jet black AB crystal bicone beads, 4 mm diameter

Marigold crystal bicone beads, 4 mm diameter

Rutilated smoky quartz teardrop-shaped beads, 8 x 6 mm

2 headpins

Chain

2 jump rings

Clasp

What You Do

1 Cut a 1½-inch piece of the 24-gauge wire. Grasp the wire ½ inch from the end with the round-nose pliers, make a small loop by wrapping the wire around one of the prongs of the pliers, then slip the wire through one of the bottom loops of the marcasite finding. Wrap the remaining wire end two to three times around the base of the loop, and trim any excess wire.

2 Slide a jet black AB bicone bead onto the wire, then add a marigold crystal bicone bead. Make a loop in the opposite end of the wire with the pliers, then add a smoky quartz bead. Wrap the remaining wire two to three times between the loop and the last bead, trimming any excess wire. Repeat steps 1 and 2 four more times, or as many times as it takes to fill out the bottom and outside loops of the marcasite finding.

3 String a marigold crystal bicone bead onto one of the headpins, make a loop in the end of the pin with the pliers, and slip it through one of the interior holes of the marcasite finding. Wrap the wire two to three times between the loop and the bead, and trim the wire as necessary. Repeat this step with a jet black AB bicone bead, slipping the pin through the remaining interior hole of the finding.

4 Cut two 3-inch pieces of the chain and a 1½-inch piece of the 24-gauge wire. Make a loop in one end of the wire and slide it through the top connecting loop of the marcasite finding. Wrap the remaining wire end two to three times around the base of the loop, and trim the wire as necessary. Then add a jet black AB bead to the wire, make a loop in the opposite end, and slip this loop through the center link of the chain length. Wrap the wire two to three times between the loop and the bead, then trim any excess wire.

5 Cut a 2-inch piece of the 24-gauge wire, make a loop in one end of the wire with the round-nose pliers, then slip the wire through an end link of the chain from step 4. Wrap the wire two to three times around the base of the loop, and trim any excess wire. Add a marigold crystal bead, a jet black AB crystal bicone bead, and another marigold crystal bead to the wire. Then make a loop in the opposite end of the wire, and then thread it through an end link of the second chain length. Wrap the remaining wire two to three times between the loop and the last bead, and trim any excess wire. Repeat this step on the opposite side of the necklace.

6 Repeat step 5 two more times. Then open one of the jump rings and slip the ring through one of the remaining end links. Close the jump ring to secure it to the necklace. Add another jump ring to the other side in the same fashion, this time slipping the bottom loop of the clasp onto the jump ring before closing it.

When Coco Chanel made costume jewelry chic during the early part of the 20th century, the mineral marcasite—also known as white iron pyrite—rose to the level of high fashion. Today, the twinkling marcasite necklaces and earrings you see in stores are created by combining the mineral with sterling silver.

To make the earrings:

What You Need

Basic tool kit (page 17)

24-gauge wire

Marcasite findings

6 jet black AB crystal bicone beads, 4 mm diameter

5 marigold crystal bicone beads, 4 mm diameter

5 smoky quartz teardrop-shaped beads, 8 x 6 mm

2 earring wires

What You Do

1 Cut a 1½-inch piece of the 24-gauge wire, then grasp the wire ½ inch from the end with the round-nose pliers, and make a small loop by wrapping the wire around one of the prongs of the pliers. Slip the wire through one of the bottom loops of one of the marcasite findings. Wrap the remaining wire end two to three times around the base of the loop, and trim any excess wire.

2 Slide a jet black AB bicone bead onto the wire, then add a marigold crystal bicone bead. Make a loop in the opposite end of the wire with the pliers, add a smoky quartz teardrop-shaped bead, and wrap the remaining wire two to three times between the loop and the last bead. Trim any excess wire. Repeat steps 1 and 2 four more times, or as many times as it takes to fill out the bottom and outside loops of the marcasite finding.

3 Cut a 1½-inch piece of the 24-gauge wire, make a loop in one end, then slide the wire through the top connecting loop of the marcasite finding. Wrap the remaining wire end two to three times at the base of the loop, and trim the wire as necessary. Add a jet black AB bead to the wire and make a loop in the opposite end, then slip this loop through the bottom loop of one of the earring wires. Wrap the wire two to three times between the loop and the bead, and trim any excess wire. Repeat the process to make the second earring.

Spring Fling Braided Necklace

This cheerful bead and ribbon necklace adds romance to any outfit.

The bright silver blossom and bold colors evoke the spirit of spring.

What You Need

Basic tool kit (page 17)

60 inches of organza ribbon,
¼ inch wide

All-purpose glue or cement

2 cord tips

10 beads with large holes

Clear nylon beading line,
40 inches long

16 to 20 crimp beads

2 jump rings, 4 mm diameter

3 jump rings, 8 mm diameter

12 to 14 small beads

30 seed beads

Large flower pendant

Bail

Clasp

Chain for necklace extender
(optional)

Headpin, 2 inches long, for
necklace extender (optional)

28-gauge silver wire for threading beads, optional

What You Do

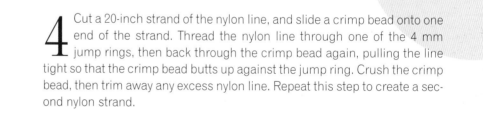

1   Cut three 20-inch strands of the organza ribbon, then tie the strands together at one end in a very tight knot. If necessary, clean up the edges of the knotted end by trimming them.

2   Apply a small drop of all-purpose glue or cement to the inside of one of the cord tips. Place the knotted end of the ribbon between the open sides of the cord tip, making sure the hole of the cord tip is pointed away from the knotted end. Use the needle-nose pliers to fold one side of the cord tip firmly over the knot, squeezing until the knot is completely pressed between the side and back of the cord tip. Repeat this process with the other side of the cord tip.

3   String five of the large-holed beads onto the first half of the ribbon lengths, dispersing the beads between the three separate strands. Make sure the beads stop 8 inches from the knot.

4   Cut a 20-inch strand of the nylon line, and slide a crimp bead onto one end of the strand. Thread the nylon line through one of the 4 mm jump rings, then back through the crimp bead again, pulling the line tight so that the crimp bead butts up against the jump ring. Crush the crimp bead, then trim away any excess nylon line. Repeat this step to create a second nylon strand.

5   Open one of the 8 mm jump rings with the needle-nose pliers, and slide both nylon strands onto it via the 4 mm jump rings. Then slide the loop from the organza ribbon's cord tip onto the 8mm jump ring, and close the jump ring.

tip —●◆●—

If you have a difficult time stringing the beads onto the gathered strands of this necklace, try making your own needle for threading. Cut a 4-inch length of the 28-gauge wire, then place the ribbon you're working with at the center of the wire and fold the wire in half over the ribbon. You've just created a needle that will make threading the beads onto the ribbon much, much easier!

6 Slide a crimp bead onto one of the nylon strands, positioning the bead so that it's 1 inch away from the crushed crimp bead at the end. Then crush this crimp bead. Slide one of the small beads onto the strand, making sure it adjoins the just-crushed crimp bead. Thread another crimp bead onto the strand, up against the small bead, and crush it so that the small bead is now locked into its place on the strand.

7 Using the crimping process from step 6, position several small beads and seed beads along the two strands of nylon line, making sure to stop the beading 8 inches from the crimped end of the strand.

8 Carefully braid and intertwine the first 8 inches of the ribbon and the first 8 inches of the nylon strands of the necklace. Now gently slide the pendant onto all the strands until it comes to rest at the 8-inch mark. (See the tip at left.) If your pendant's hole isn't large enough to accommodate all the strands, add a bail to it.

9 Repeat step 3 and steps 6 through 8 with the second half of the necklace. After braiding all of the strands, gather the three ends of the organza ribbon together and tie a secure knot 8 inches from the pendant. Trim any excess ribbon. Then repeat step 2 with the second cord tip.

10 Repeat the crimping process from step 4 with the remaining end of the nylon lines. Then repeat step 5 to attach the nylon and the ribbon strands together via the 8 mm jump ring, this time adding the clasp to the jump ring as well.

11 If desired, make a necklace extender by cutting a 1 ½-inch piece of the chain. Open the remaining 4 mm jump ring, and slip it through one end of the chain and through the 4 mm jump ring on the end of the necklace opposite the clasp. Then close the jump ring.

12 To complete the extender, slide a bead or two onto the headpin. Grasp the end of the pin with the round-nose pliers, and wrap the wire around one of the prongs of the pliers to form a small loop. Slide this loop through the other end of the silver chain. Wrap any remaining wire around the pin between the bottom of the loop and the top of the bead using the needle-nose pliers.

Flowers-on-the-Side Choker

Few necklaces draw attention to the face more rapturously than this choker. The floral focal point is a genuine rose, perfectly preserved.

What You Need

Basic tool kit (page 17)

Tigertail wire

Crimp beads

6 silver beads, 4 x 2 mm

114 white freshwater pearls, 4 mm diameter

19 oblong crystal beads, 6 x 4 mm

36 rondele glass beads, 6 x 4 mm

6 spacer bars

18 oblong ceramic beads, 6 x 4 mm

2 end spacers

4 jump rings, 8 mm diameter

2 to 4 jump rings (depending on the number required to attach the strands to the back of the flower pendant), 4 mm diameter

Preserved flower pendant, 40 to 50 mm diameter

Silver chain (optional, for necklace extender)

Clasp

Headpin (optional, for necklace extender)

What You Do

1 To create the first section of the necklace, cut three 8-inch pieces of the tigertail wire with the craft scissors, then take one of the pieces and string beads onto it in the following order:

1 crimp bead
1 silver bead
5 freshwater pearls
1 crystal bead
1 rondele bead

2 Thread the wire through the top hole of one of the spacer bars, then add the following beads to the wire:

1 rondele bead
1 crystal bead
6 pearls
1 ceramic bead
1 rondele bead

3 Thread the wire through the top hole of a second spacer bar, then add the following beads to the wire:

1 rondele bead
1 ceramic bead
1 pearl
1 crimp bead

4 Repeat steps 1 through 3 with an 8-inch piece of wire, but thread this piece through the bottom hole of the spacer bars instead of the top hole.

5 String the following beads onto the third 8-inch piece of wire:

1 crimp bead
1 silver bead
5 pearls
1 rondele bead
1 ceramic bead

Thread the wire through the central hole of the first spacer bar, then add beads to the wire in this order:

1 ceramic bead
1 rondele bead
6 pearls
1 rondele bead
1 crystal bead

6 Slide the wire through the central hole of the second spacer bar and add the following beads:

1 crystal bead
1 rondele bead
1 pearl
1 crimp bead

7 Take the first strand of wire and thread the end with the silver bead through the first loop of one of the end spacers. Wind the wire around and back through the crimp bead and the silver bead, then pull the end of the wire until the crimp bead butts up against the end spacer. Crimp the bead using the needle-nose pliers, and trim away any excess wire with the scissors.

8 Repeat step 7 on the opposite end of the strand, this time sliding the wire through an 8 mm jump ring before crimping. Pull the wire tight before crimping so that no gaps remain between the beads. Repeat steps 7 and 8 with the other two 8-inch strands.

9 Use the needle-nose pliers to open a 4 mm jump ring, then slide the ring onto one of the 8 mm jump rings with the beaded strands. Slip the smaller jump ring through a loop at the back of the flower pendant, and close the ring securely with the pliers. If your pendant has a second loop on this side, repeat this step.

10 To make the second part of the necklace, cut three 12-inch pieces of the tigertail wire. Take one of the pieces and string beads onto it in the following order:

1 pearl
1 crystal bead
1 rondele bead

11 Thread the wire through the top hole of one of the spacer bars, then add the following beads to the wire:

1 rondele bead
1 crystal bead
7 pearls
1 ceramic bead
1 rondele bead

12 Thread the wire through the top hole of a second spacer bar, then add the following beads to the wire:

1 rondele bead
1 ceramic bead
7 pearls
1 crystal bead
1 rondele bead

13 Thread the wire through the top hole of a third spacer bar, then add the following beads to the wire:

1 rondele bead
1 crystal bead
6 pearls
1 ceramic bead
1 rondele bead

14 Thread the wire through the top hole of a fourth spacer bar, then add the following beads:

1 rondele bead
1 ceramic bead
5 pearls
1 silver bead
1 crimp bead

15 Repeat steps 10 through 14 with another 8-inch piece of wire, threading this one through the bottom holes of the spacer bars. Then string the following beads onto the third 8-inch piece of wire:

1 pearl
1 rondele bead
1 ceramic bead

16 Thread the wire through the central hole of the first spacer bar, then add the following beads to the wire:

1 ceramic bead
1 rondele bead
7 pearls
1 rondele bead
1 crystal bead

17 Slide the wire through the central hole of the second spacer bar, then add the following beads to the wire:

1 crystal bead
1 rondele bead
7 pearls
1 rondele bead
1 ceramic bead

18 Thread the wire through the center of the third spacer bar, then add the following beads to the wire:

1 ceramic bead
1 rondele bead
6 pearls
1 rondele bead
1 crystal bead

19 Thread the wire through the fourth spacer bar, then add the following beads:

1 crystal bead
1 rondele bead
5 pearls
1 silver bead
1 crimp bead

20 Take the first strand from this group and thread the end with the silver bead through the first loop of the second end spacer. Wind the wire around and back through the crimp bead and the silver bead, then pull the end of the wire until the crimp bead butts up against the end spacer. Crimp the bead using the needle-nose pliers, and trim away any excess wire with the scissors.

21 Repeat Step 20 on the opposite end of the strand, this time sliding the wire through an 8 mm jump ring before crimping. Pull the wire tight before crimping so that no gaps remain between the beads. Then repeat steps 20 and 21 with the other two strands.

22 Using the needle-nose pliers, open a 4 mm jump ring and slide it onto the 8 mm jump ring with the beaded strands. Slip the smaller jump ring through a loop at the back of the flower pendant, then close the ring securely with the pliers. If your pendant has a second loop on this side of the pendant, repeat this step.

23 Using the needle-nose pliers, open an 8 mm jump ring and slip it through the top loop of an end spacer and then through the jump ring. Close the jump ring with the pliers. Open the remaining 8 mm jump ring with the pliers, and wind it through the top loop of the other end spacer. Close the jump ring to complete the necklace.

24 If desired, make a necklace extender by cutting a 3-inch piece of the silver chain with the wire cutters. Open the 8 mm jump ring on the end spacer on the end of the necklace without the clasp. Slip the jump ring through one end of the chain, and close the jump ring with the pliers.

25 To complete the extender, slide a crystal bead onto the headpin, grasp the end of the pin with the round-nose pliers and make a small loop in the wire. Slide this loop through the remaining end of the silver chain. Use the needle-nose pliers to wrap any remaining wire around the pin between the bottom of the loop and the top of the bead.

Dramatic

There's no mistaking a dramatic flare, in this or any other age. It all comes down to spellbinding color, dynamic shapes, and a derring-do attitude. Just consider the divas who've graced stage and screen—there's not a drab personality or bland bauble among them. Now it's your turn to take center stage with the dramatic designs in this chapter.

Chinese Bi Set

The small disks featured here, called bi, were used as ceremonial pieces in ancient China. Today, they make a lasting and colorful impression in jewelry design.

To make the necklace:
What You Need

Basic tool kit (page 17)

Black cord

2 crimp beads

Clasp

Jump ring

3 carnelian round beads, 10 mm diameter

Coin with center hole, 25 mm diameter

Disk-shaped bead, 50 mm diameter

Tidbit:

Jade disks like these were sometimes buried with Chinese aristocrats during the Han Dynasty, between the third centuries BC and AD. The disks were placed on the chest and beneath the head and feet of the deceased. Though their exact meaning is unknown, it is thought that because dragons were sometimes carved into the disks, they were probably meant to aid the dead as they moved from this world into the next.

What You Do

1 Cut three 20-inch pieces of the black cord, then slide a crimp bead around all three pieces at one end. Thread the gathered cords through the ring part of the clasp, then back through the crimp bead. Pull the cord until the crimp bead butts up tightly against the clasp, then crush the crimp bead. Repeat this step, this time using the jump ring instead of the clasp.

Figure 1

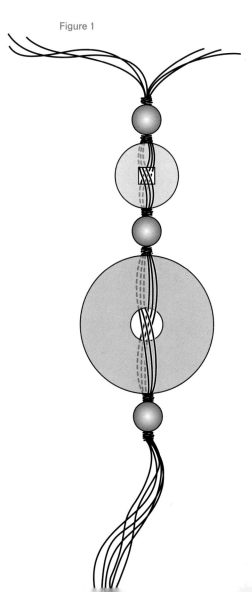

2 Make a simple knot with all 6 pieces of cord about 8½ inches from the crimp beads (see figure 1). Slide one of the carnelian round beads onto the knotted bunch of cord, placing the bead against the knot. Then form another knot on the opposite side of the bead, making sure that the carnelian bead rests securely between both knots.

3 Split the cords in half at the base of the second knot, and slide the coin between the cords. Weave three cords from the front to the back via the center hole. Then weave the other three cords from the back to the front in the same fashion. Gather all six pieces of cord at the base of the coin and tie another knot, making sure that the coin rests securely between the two knots.

4 Thread another carnelian bead onto the knotted bunch of cord, and knot it into place. Split the cords in half at the base of this knot, and slide the disk-shaped bead between the cords. Then weave the disk onto the necklace in the same way as the coin, and make a knot at the base of the disk.

5 Slide the last carnelian bead onto the knotted bunch of cord. Form another knot, making sure it holds the bead tightly in place. Allow the remaining cord to dangle. Trim any excess cord.

To make the earrings:

What You Need

Basic tool kit (page 17)

22-gauge gold-filled wire

2 disk-shaped beads, 20 mm

2 carnelian round beads, 10 mm

2 earring wires

What You Do

1 Cut a 2-inch piece of the 22-gauge wire, slide one of the disk-shaped beads to the center of the wire, and gently fold the wire around it. Then thread both ends of the wire through a carnelian round bead.

2 Wrap one end of the wire two times at the top of the carnelian bead, making sure that the bead and the disk rest securely together. Then use the round-nose pliers to form a loop in the other end of the wire, about ½ inch from the end. Slide this loop through the loop at the base of an earring wire, then wrap the remaining wire two to three times between the base of the loop and the previously wrapped wire. Trim any excess wire. Repeat the process to make the other earring.

Silver Wrap Harlequin Set

These matching black-and-white pieces were inspired by harlequins.

The curves and the color scheme echo the jaunty grace of the classic clowns.

What You Need

Basic tool kit (page 17)

18-gauge sterling silver wire

3 large black buttons with 2 holes apiece, or flat beads with large center holes

3 large clear buttons with 2 holes apiece, or flat beads with large center holes

3 large white buttons with 2 holes apiece, or flat beads with large center holes

What You Do

tip

The length of wire required for both of these projects may vary according to the size of your wrist and finger.

1 Cut a 20-inch piece of the 18-gauge wire, fold the wire in half, and create a loop at the center. Then twist the wire sides together beneath this loop two to three times.

2 Cut a 40-inch piece of the 18-gauge wire, and thread this wire through the loop made in step 1 until the loop rests at the center of the 40-inch wire. Then fold the 40-inch wire in half inside the loop and draw it down next to the wires leading from the loop.

3 There should now be a total of four lengths of wire leading from the loop: the two shorter lengths of wire from step 1 and the two longer lengths from step 2. Wrap one of the longest lengths of wire tightly around the other wires four to six times, then bring the four lengths together again, side by side.

4 Slide a large black button onto the two longest lengths of wire, about 1 inch from where the wire was wrapped in step 3. Add a clear button and a white button. Allow the two shortest lengths of wire to pass beneath the buttons, then use the needle-nose pliers and your fingertips to wrap the wire ends in a spiral pattern on top of the ring four to six times.

5 Now draw the longest wire from the top down and around the buttons in the direction of the wire loop. Wrap this wire three to five times around all four lengths of wire, next to the button. Now pull this wire beneath the buttons so that it joins the two shortest lengths.

6 Draw the other wire from the top around the buttons, away from the wire loop made in step 1. Wrap this wire three to five times around all four lengths of wire on the opposite side of the buttons. Then straighten the wire so that it joins the other three lengths.

7 Repeat steps 4 through 6 two additional times, this time adding the buttons ¾ to 1¼ inches from where the wire was wrapped in step 6, depending on the desired size of the bracelet.

8 Fold the longest remaining piece of wire in half approximately 1¾ to 2¼ inches from the last wire wrapping, depending on the desired size. Bend this wire ¼ to ½ inch from the top around the round-nose pliers to form a hook. Wrap this wire two to three times around the others, then trim away any excess wire. Then wrap each remaining wire two times around the other wires to secure the bracelet together. Trim each piece with the wire cutters, then wrap the next length of wire on top of the cut to disguise it.

To make the ring:

What You Need

Basic tool kit (page 17)

18-gauge sterling silver wire

**1 large black button with 2 holes,
or 1 flat bead with a large center hole**

**1 large white button with 2 holes,
or 1 flat bead with a large center hole**

**1 large clear button with 2 holes,
or 1 flat bead with a large center hole**

What You Do

1 Cut a 20-inch piece of the 18-gauge wire, wrap the wire two to three times around the ring mandrel or the dowel, then thread the ends of the wire through all three of the buttons, so that the ends emerge from the top of the ring.

2 Use the needle-nose pliers and your fingertips to wrap the wire ends four to six times in a spiral pattern on top of the ring. Then draw the remaining wire down and around the buttons to the wire ring underneath. Wrap the wires four to six times around the wire ring on each side. Trim any excess wire.

Tidbit:

During the Renaissance, people often wore rings on all 10 fingers, sometimes adding more than one ring to each finger. In fact, so many were worn that officials in Florence issued a decree in 1415 limiting the number of rings and gemstones a woman might wear on her hands.

Celestial Necklace

Try using romantic materials, like this dreamy strand of organza, to display your favorite beads and pendants. Here, the black ribbon and silver sun form a striking juxtaposition.

What You Need

Basic tool kit (page 17)

15 inches of organza ribbon, ½ inch wide

Pendant

Bail (optional)

2 jump rings

2 cord tips

Clasp

Tidbit:

Designs like the sterling silver sun used here were popular during the reign of Louis XIV. (He was, after all, known as the Sun King.) Throughout the 17th century in France, celestial motifs, as well as ribbons and bows, held sway among the fashionable.

What You Do

1 Slide the pendant to the center of the ribbon, using the bail, if desired.

2 Open one of the jump rings, slide it through the loop of one of the cord tips, then close the jump ring. Repeat this step, this time sliding the clasp onto the jump ring before closing it.

3 Carefully fold one tip of the organza ribbon and slide it in between the open sides of one of the cord tips. Use the needle-nose pliers to fold one side of the cord tip over the ribbon, squeezing until the ribbon is completely pressed between the side and back of the cord tip. Repeat with the other side of the cord tip, then repeat this step with the other side of the organza ribbon to complete the necklace.

tip

The color of your organza ribbon doesn't have to match your pendant. Look for a ribbon that complements the piece.

Blue Cloisonné Beaded Choker and Bracelet

No matter what the decade, cloisonné always seems to be in fashion. The traditional enamel beads, complemented here by accents of red and blue, give this set a vintage feel.

To make the necklace:

What You Need

Basic tool kit (page 17)

24-gauge wire

Pen or thin dowel

6 pale blue crystal bicone beads, 4 mm diameter

10 Indian sapphire crystal bicone beads, 6 mm diameter

10 bead caps

4 cloisonné beads, 22 x 15 mm

1 cloisonné bead, 30 x 20 mm

32-gauge wire

Red seed beads

20 inches of velvet ribbon, 1 inch wide

Fray retardant

Jump ring

Clasp

What You Do

1 Cut a 9-inch piece of the 24-gauge wire, make a large loop approximately ¾ inch from one end by wrapping the wire around a pen or thin dowel. Wrap the remaining wire end two to three times at the base of the loop, and trim any excess wire.

2 String a pale blue crystal bead onto the wire, followed by an Indian sapphire bead, a bead cap, a 22 x 15 mm cloisonné bead, a second bead cap, and another Indian sapphire bead.

3 Repeat the beading pattern in step 2. Now reverse the beading pattern for two additional repetitions so that there are two Indian sapphire crystal beads at the center of the beading pattern. Now add one more pale blue crystal bicone. Follow the instructions in step 1 to create and secure a large loop in the remaining end of the wire.

4 Cut a 3 ½-inch piece of the 24-gauge wire. Grasp the wire ½ inch from one end with the round-nose pliers. Make a small loop by winding the wire around one of the prongs, and slip it between the two Indian sapphire crystal bicone beads at the center of the necklace. Wrap the remaining wire end two to three times at the base of the loop, trimming any excess wire with the wire cutters as necessary.

5 Add a pale blue crystal bicone, an Indian sapphire bead, a bead cap, the 30 x 20 mm cloisonné bead, a second bead cap, another Indian sapphire bead, and a pale blue crystal bead. Use the round-nose pliers to make a small loop in the end of the wire, and wrap the remaining wire two to three times between this loop and the last bead.

6 Cut a 2 ½-inch piece of the 32-gauge wire, make a small loop in one end with the round-nose pliers, and slip it through the bottom loop in the wire beneath the large cloisonné bead. Thread 1¼ inches of red seed beads onto the strand, then fold the wire in half and thread it back through the seed beads. Wrap the remaining wire three to four times between the top loop and the first seed bead. Trim

Tidbit:

The art of cloisonné enameling originated in thirteenth century Japan and has experienced several flowerings in popularity over the centuries. In the late 1800s, thanks in part to the exacting work of Peter Carl Fabergé, who was known for his jewelry designs and for his famous Fabergé eggs, the art form reached new heights of refinement. It was also very much in vogue during the Art Deco period.

any excess wire, then repeat this step two to five times, depending on the amount of beaded fringe desired.

7 Cut the velvet ribbon into two 10-inch pieces, fold one of the lengths in half, and carefully thread it through the large loop at one end of the necklace. Repeat with the other side, then apply a fray retardant to the ends, if desired.

8 Cut a 10-inch length from the 24-gauge wire. Using the pen or thin dowel, make a large loop at the center of the wire. Make two twists beneath the loop, and then wrap both sides of the wire carefully around the end of the velvet ribbon. Tuck the ends inside the wire wrapping to hide them.

9 Attach a jump ring to the clasp, and then repeat step 7 on the other side of the necklace, this time slipping the jump ring and clasp onto the large loop before closing it.

tip ‑‑●●●‑

Both the French and the Russians are known for their cloisonné beads. The addition of fringe beneath the pendant is a hallmark of the Russian style. The fringe is often made of chain or beaded wire.

To make the bracelet:

What You Need

Basic tool kit (page 17)

Tigertail wire

10 Indian sapphire crystal bicone beads, 6 mm diameter

10 bead caps

3 cloisonné beads, 22 x 15 mm

5 pale blue crystal bicone beads, 4 mm diameter

2 cloisonné beads, 30 x 20 mm

2 crimp beads

Jump ring

Clasp

What You Do

1 Cut a 13-inch piece of the tiger-tail wire, then string an Indian sapphire bead onto the wire, followed by a bead cap, a 22 x 15 mm cloisonné bead, a second bead cap, an Indian sapphire bead, and a pale blue crystal bicone bead. Repeat this beading pattern, this time using a 30 x 20 mm cloisonné bead.

2 Repeat the entire beading pattern from step 1. Then repeat the first part of the beading pattern. Once you've added the pale blue crystal bead, add a crimp bead to both ends of the wire.

3 Thread one wire end through the jump ring, then back through the crimp bead and the first crystal bead. Pull the wire until it's tight, then crush the crimp bead, and trim any excess wire. Repeat the crimping process on the opposite side of the bracelet, this time substituting the clasp for the jump ring.

Waves of Pearls Necklace and Bracelet

Green, a color that was fashionable during the Victorian era, is featured in this dramatic design. You'll find that green comes in an incredible array of shades, including emerald, avocado, and aventurine.

What You Need

Basic tool kit (page 17)

55 headpins

92 round freshwater pearls, 6 mm

64 bicone crystal AB beads, 4 mm

36 bicone crystal beads, 6 mm

24-gauge gold wire

Gold chain

1 jump ring

Clasp

What You Do

1 Slide a freshwater pearl onto one of the headpins, then add a 4 mm bicone bead. Grasp the end of the headpin with the round-nose pliers, and make a small loop in the wire. Wrap the remaining wire around the pin two to three times between the bottom of the loop and the top of the bead using the needle-nose pliers. Trim any excess wire, then repeat this step 18 more times.

2 Thread a 4 mm bicone bead onto one of the headpins, then add two pearls and a 6 mm bicone bead. Follow the procedure in step 1 to form a wrapped loop at the top. Repeat this step 18 more times.

3 Slide a 6 mm bicone bead onto a headpin, followed by two 4 mm bicone beads. Form a loop in the end of the headpin with the round-nose pliers, then slide one of the headpins from step 2 onto this loop. Wrap any remain-ing wire beneath the bottom of the loop using the needle-nose pliers, and trim away any excess wire. Repeat this step 9 more times.

4 Thread a 6 mm crystal bead onto another headpin, then add a 4 mm bicone bead. Form a loop in the end of the head-pin with the round-nose pliers, slide one of the headpins from step 2 onto this loop, and wrap any remaining wire beneath the bottom of the loop using the needle-nose pliers. Trim any excess wire with the wire cutters, then repeat this step 9 more times.

5 Cut a 24-inch piece of the 24-gauge wire with the wire cut-ters. Grasp one end of the wire with the round-nose pliers, and follow the procedure in step 1 to create a wrapped loop.

6 Slide a pearl onto this wire. Thread the wire through the loop of one of the headpins from step 1, then add another pearl. Now add a headpin from step 3 by looping the 24-gauge wire once between the two pearls on the headpin and pulling it taut. Repeat this step, except replace the head-pin from step 3 with a headpin from step 4.

7 Repeat step 6 three more times. Cut a 1-inch piece of the gold chain and a 1½-inch piece of the 24-gauge wire. Grasp the wire ½ inch from one end with the round-nose pliers, and form a small loop. Wrap the remaining wire two to three times beneath this loop using the needle-nose pliers. Trim any extra wire.

8 Slide a pearl and then a 4 mm bicone bead onto the wire. Using the round-nose pliers, form a loop in the other end of the wire. Slip one end of the chain onto this loop, then wrap the remaining wire two to three times between the loop and the beads with the needle-nose pliers. Trim any extra wire.

9 Slide a 4 mm bicone bead onto a headpin, then add two pearls and a 6 mm bicone bead. Grasp the end of the headpin with the round-nose pliers, and form a small loop. Slip this loop through the other end of the chain length. Wrap the remaining wire around the pin two to three times between the bottom of the loop and the top of the bead, using the needle-nose pliers, and trim any excess wire.

10 Thread the piece from step 9 onto the necklace via the top loop. Then repeat step 6 four additional times.

11 Grasp one end of the wire with the round-nose pliers, and form a small loop. Wrap the remaining wire around the pin two to three times between the bottom of the loop and the top of the bead, using the needle-nose pliers. Trim any excess wire.

12 Open one of the jump rings, slip it through the loop at one end of the necklace, and close the ring. Then open the jump ring attached to the clasp, slide it through the wire loop at the opposite end of the necklace, and close the ring. If you like, you can add an extender to the necklace. Refer to step 00 on page 000 for instructions.

To make the bracelet:

What You Need

Basic tool kit (page 17)

40 round freshwater pearls, 6 mm

30 bicone crystal AB beads, 4 mm

30 headpins

10 bicone crystal beads, 6 mm

24-gauge gold wire

Clasp

What You Do

1 Thread a freshwater pearl and a 4 mm bicone bead onto one of the headpins, grasp the end of the headpin with the round-nose pliers, and make a small loop in the wire. Wrap the remaining wire around the pin two to three times between the bottom of the loop and the top of the bead, using the needle-nose pliers. Then trim away any excess wire. Repeat this step nine more times.

2 Thread two pearls onto a headpin, and follow the procedure in step 1 to form a wrapped loop at the top. Repeat this step nine additional times.

3 Thread a 4 mm bicone bead, a 6 mm bicone bead, and another 4 mm bicone bead onto a headpin. Grasp the end of the headpin with the round-nose pliers, and make a small loop in the wire. Slide one of the headpins from step 2 onto this loop, then use the needle-nose pliers to wrap any remaining wire beneath the bottom of the loop. Trim away any excess wire, then repeat this step four additional times.

4 Thread a 6 mm crystal bead and a 4 mm bicone bead onto a headpin. Grasp the end of the headpin with the round-nose pliers, form a small loop, and slide one of the headpins from step 2 onto this loop. Then wrap any remaining wire beneath the bottom of the loop using the needle-nose pliers. Trim away any excess wire with the wire cutters, then repeat this step four additional times.

5 Cut a 15-inch piece of the 24-gauge wire, grasp one end of the wire with the round-nose pliers, and follow the procedure from step 1 to create a wrapped loop.

6 Slide a pearl onto the wire, thread the wire through the loop of one of the headpins from step 1, then add another pearl. Add one of the headpins from step 3 by looping the 24-gauge wire once between the two pearls on the headpin and pulling it tight. Repeat this step, replacing the headpin from step 3 with a headpin from step 4. Repeat this step four additional times.

7 Form a wrapped loop with the end of the wire by repeating the procedure in step 1, this time threading the clasp onto the loop before wrapping the wire. Trim away any excess wire.

Shimmering Headband

This vintage-inspired velvet headband will make you feel regal and refined.

To wear it, simply tie the ends together at the nape of your neck.

What You Need

Basic tool kit (page 17)

18-gauge wire

Red firepolish crystal beads, 8 mm diameter

2 jump rings

20 inches of velvet ribbon, ¼ inch wide

24-gauge wire

What You Do

1 Cut a 5-inch strand of the 18-gauge wire, and use the round-nose pliers to make a small loop in one end of the strand. Then make a larger, oblong loop along the side of and perpendicular to the first loop. Make a smaller loop, similar to the first, along the side of the larger loop, and finish out the elongated clover shape with a second oblong loop. Trim any excess wire, then repeat this step 10 more times.

2 Cut a 1-inch piece of the 18-gauge wire, and make a loop in one end with the round-nose pliers. Slide a red firepolish crystal bead onto the other end of the wire, and make a loop on the opposite side. Hook this loop through one of the oblong loops of the clover shape. Then close the loop of the beaded wire tightly around the oblong to secure the two together.

3 Cut another 1-inch piece of the 18-gauge wire, make a loop in one end with the round-nose pliers, and hook it through the other long loop of the clover from step 2. Close the loop of the wire securely, then slide a red firepolish crystal bead onto the other end. Repeat steps 2 and 3 ten more times.

4 Slide a jump ring through the loop of the beaded wire on one end of the headband and close it firmly. Cut the velvet ribbon in half, thread one end through the jump ring, and fold it over about ½ inch.

5 Cut a 4-inch piece of the 24-gauge wire, then use the needle-nose pliers to wrap the wire around the folded ribbon several times to secure it to the jump ring. Trim any excess wire, then tuck the wire ends between the fold of the ribbon.

6 Repeat steps 4 and 5 on the other side. Refer to step 2 to make two more beaded wires, but this time, attach one to the other end of the cord or ribbon. Fold the ribbon over and secure it using the 24-gauge wire, as in step 5. Repeat on the other side.

Eye-Popping Flower Necklace

Inspired by bakelite jewelry pieces from the 1930s and 40s, this bold

beaded flower necklace glitters with retro style.

What You Need

Basic tool kit (page 17)

Tigertail wire

2 crimp beads

Toggle clasp

2 silver beads, 6 x 4 mm

Freshwater pearls,
6 mm diameter

24-gauge silver wire

5 large teardrop-shaped beads,
25 x 15 mm

Jump ring

tip —◆◆◆—

If the 24-gauge wire is too thick to fit through your teardrop beads, try 26-gauge wire instead. It's thinner but sturdy enough to hold the shape of the flower without breaking.

What You Do

1 Cut a 20-inch piece of the tigertail wire, and slide a crimp bead onto one end of the strand. Then attach one side of the toggle clasp by threading the end of the wire through the loop of the clasp. Thread the wire back through the crimp bead, crush the crimp bead with the needle-nose pliers, and trim away any excess wire.

2 String one silver bead onto the tigertail wire, then add 20 inches of pearls, another silver bead, and a crimp bead. Attach the other side of the toggle clasp to the wire by threading the end of the wire through the loop of the clasp. Then thread the wire back through the crimp bead and pull the end of the wire until the crimp bead butts up against the clasp's loop. Crush the crimp bead, and trim away any excess wire.

3 To make the flower, cut a 40-inch piece of the 24-gauge wire, and thread the five large teardrop-shaped beads onto the center of the strand. Draw the sides of the wire toward each other to pull the teardrop beads into a circle, and form the flower shape.

4 To secure the pendant's shape, weave the sides of the wire around the base of the teardrop beads at the center of the flower. Do this at least twice with both sides of the wire for a total of four wraps around each bead.

5 Pull both sides of the wire through the center of the flower, and string 10 to 15 pearls of various sizes onto the strand. Wind the two beaded wires around each other to make the front of the flower. Then thread the wires back through the center of the flower, to what is now the back of the flower pendant.

6 Wind the two pieces of bare wire tightly together three or four times at the back of the pendant to secure the pearls. Then thread these joined wires under the wire wrapping at the base of one of the teardrop beads.

7 Using the round-nose pliers, create a loop with the joined wires and slip it through the jump ring. Wrap the remaining wires two to three times around the base of the loop, and trim away any excess wire. Then open the jump ring and slide it around the center of the strand of pearls, and close the jump ring.

Tidbit

Pearls form naturally. When a grain of sand intrudes inside an oyster, the oyster coats the grain with nacre, also called mother of pearl, a compound that smoothes over the irritant. Over time, that grain of sand becomes a pearl— lustrous, round, and perfect. Natural pearls were once so rare, they were considered the most valuable jewel in the world. Natural freshwater pearls form in mussels, not oysters. Cultured freshwater pearls can produce colors unseen in saltwater pearls.

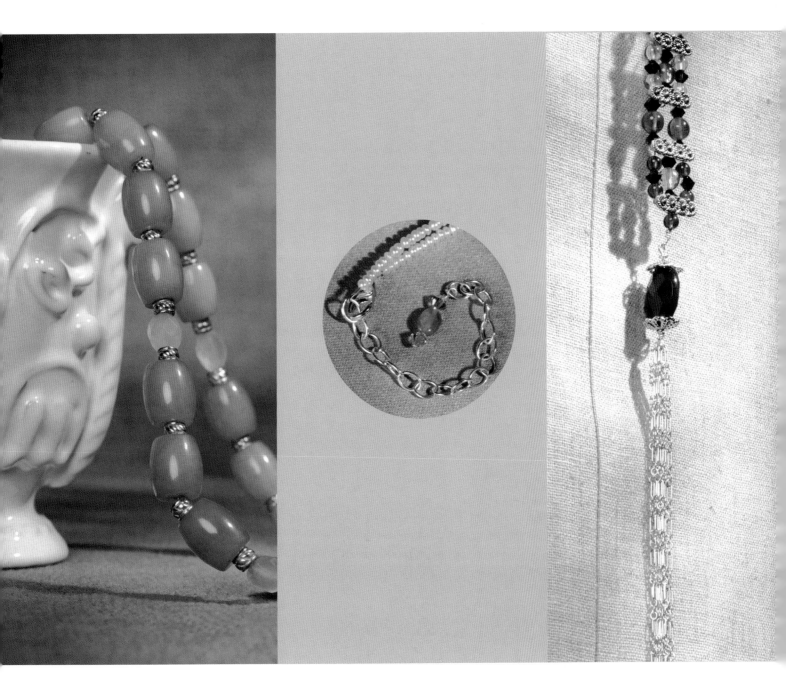

Elegant

Delicate brooches, ornate pocket watches, necklaces fit for a queen—elegant jewelry can make you feel distinguished thanks to its timeless grace and charm. The pieces on the following pages were designed to draw out your inner sparkle. Add them to your wardrobe, and you'll radiate elegant style.

Neoclassical Necklace

Bringing to mind the clean designs of ancient Greece, this timeless piece is easy to put together. To make the necklace feel light and modern, use beads in subtle shades of green and blue.

What You Need

Basic tool kit (page 17)

Tigertail wire

24 Gold accent beads

19 Barrel beads, 14 x 8 mm

4 Faceted beads, 8 x 8 mm

2 crimp beads

Clasp

Jump ring or split ring

What You Do

1 Cut a 20-inch piece of the tigertail wire, then string on a gold accent bead and a barrel bead. Alternate between these two types of beads until a total of six gold accent beads and five barrel beads have been strung. Then add a faceted bead.

2 Repeat step 1, adding a faceted bead after three barrel beads and four gold beads have been strung. Then repeat this step two more times.

3 Alternate between barrel beads and gold beads again, stopping after five barrel beads and six gold beads have been strung.

4 Add a crimp bead to each end of the strand. Thread the clasp onto one end, then wind the wire around and back through the crimp bead and the first bead or two. Pull the end of the wire until the crimp bead butts up against the clasp, then crimp the bead and trim away any excess wire.

5 Repeat step 4 on the other end of the strand, substituting a jump ring for the clasp. Thread the wire through the jump ring, making sure the wire is pulled tightly enough so that no gaps remain between the beads.

Silver and Onyx Pocket Watch

Solve your punctuality problems with this pretty watch. Tuck it into a pocket,

and you'll have a new reason to obsess over time.

What You Need

Basic tool kit (page 17)

24-gauge wire

Chain

Large watch face

20 onyx round beads, 4 mm

8 smoke gray crystal bicone beads, 6 mm

Pocket clip

3 headpins

What You Do

1 Cut a 2-inch piece of the 24-gauge wire and a 1½-inch length of the chain. Using the round-nose pliers, grasp the wire ½ inch from the end and make a loop by wrapping the wire around one of the prongs of the pliers. Slip this loop through the top connecting ring or bar of the watch and wrap the wire two to three times around the base of the loop. Slide an onyx bead onto the wire, followed by a smoke gray crystal bicone bead and another onyx bead. Make a loop in the opposite end of the wire and slip it through one of the end links of the chain. Wrap the remaining wire two to three times between the loop and the last bead. Trim any excess wire.

2 Repeat step 1 three more times, but instead of sliding the first loop through the watch bar each time, slide it through the remaining end link of each length of chain. Create one more beaded wire and attach it to the chain length. Make sure the second loop of this wire is large enough to fit through and around the loop of the pocket clip.

3 Thread five onyx beads, a smoke gray crystal bicone bead, and one more onyx bead onto one of the headpins. Form a loop in the end of the pin with the round-nose pliers, then slip the loop through the bottom connecting ring of the watch face. Wrap the wire two to three times between the loop and the last bead and trim any excess wire.

4 Thread one onyx bead, one smoke gray crystal bead, and another onyx bead onto a headpin. Wrap the end of the headpin around the headpin from step 3, in between the third and fourth onyx beads, forming a loop with the round-nose pliers to secure the headpin. Repeat this step with a second headpin to complete the watch.

Tidbit:

Watches didn't come into widespread use until the mid-1700s. Prior to that era, they were wildly inaccurate and very expensive. By tradition, pocket watch chains are about nine inches long, but you can make yours as long as you like.

Delicate Drops of Amethyst Necklace

Few gemstones look more regal than the amethyst. Here, amethyst briolette beads pair up with gold chain and accents of citrine to create a necklace worthy of royalty.

What You Need

Basic tool kit (page 17)

Gold chain

24-gauge gold wire

1 amethyst briolette bead, 10 mm diameter

3 citrine beads, 6 x 8 mm

1 amethyst briolette bead, 8 mm diameter

12 amethyst briolette beads, 6 mm diameter

Jump ring or split ring

Clasp

What You Do

1. Cut a 21-inch piece and a 3-inch piece of the gold chain with the wire cutters. Then cut a 2-inch piece of the 24-gauge wire, and slide one end of the strand through the lateral hole at the top of the 10 mm amethyst briolette bead, making sure a ½-inch length of wire emerges from the other side of the bead.

2. Using your fingertips or the needle-nose pliers, pinch both sides of the wire together so that they form a triangular shape at the top of the bead. Wrap the short end of the wire two to three times around the longer end at the top of the briolette bead. Then trim any extra wire.

3. Slide a citrine bead onto the wire. Then grasp the wire with the round-nose pliers, and make a small loop in the wire. Slide this loop through the center link of the 21-inch length of gold chain. Wrap any remaining wire between the bottom of the loop and the top of the bead using the needle-nose pliers. Trim any extra wire.

4. Cut a 1½-inch piece of the gold wire, and slide one end through the top of the 8 mm amethyst briolette bead, making sure a ½-inch length of the wire emerges from the other side. Use your fingertips or the needle-nose pliers to pinch both ends of the wire together so that they form a triangular shape at the top of the bead, as in step 2. Then clip one of the wires about ⅛ inch from the top of the bead.

5. Use the round-nose pliers to form a loop in the wire above the triangle, centering the loop over the bead. Then slide the loop onto the center link of the 3-inch length of gold chain. Keeping the round-nose pliers inside the loop with one hand, use the needle-nose pliers or your fingers to wrap the longer wire between the base of the loop and the tip of the bead. Once you've reached the top of the wire triangle, trim any excess wire.

6 Cut a 2-inch piece of the 24-gauge wire. Slide one end of the wire through the lateral hole at the top of one of the 6 mm amethyst briolette beads, making sure a ½-inch length of the wire emerges from the other side. Use your fingertips or the needle-nose pliers to pinch both sides of the wire together so that they form a triangular shape at the top of the bead. Wrap the short end of the wire two to three times around the longer end at the top of the briolette, then trim any extra wire.

7 Slide a citrine bead onto the wire, then grasp the wire with the round-nose pliers and make a small loop. Slide this loop through an end link of the 3-inch length of chain. Then thread this same loop through a link approximately 3 inches from the center of the 21-inch chain length and its 10 mm briolette bead.

8 Close the loop and wrap any remaining wire between the bottom of the loop and the top

of the bead, using the needle-nose pliers. Trim any extra wire. Repeat steps 6 through 8 on the opposite sides of both chain lengths.

9 Repeat steps 4 and 5 with the remaining 6 mm briolette beads. Position two of them 1½ inches from the center of the 21-inch chain length, or midway between the briolettes from steps 1 and 6. The remainder should be placed at approximately 1-inch intervals out to the end of the necklace, though adjustments can be made according to personal design preferences.

10 Open a jump ring or split ring, slip it onto the end link of the 21-inch chain, and close it. Then open the jump ring or split ring attached to the clasp, and slide it onto the opposite end of the chain. Close the ring to complete the necklace.

Firecracker Brooch

This bright brooch will add vintage sparkle to any jacket or scarf.

2 Attach seven more medium-sized beads in the same manner to form a circular cluster in the middle of the mesh dome. After attaching the last of these beads, twist the wire ends together at the back of the mesh dome, and trim away any excess wire.

3 Cut a 12-inch piece of the 26-gauge wire, then thread one end of the wire through the center of the mesh dome, so that the wire emerges in the middle of the cluster of beads from step 2. Thread one of the seed beads onto the wire in the front, then thread it through to the back, pulling the wire until it's tight. Thread the wire through to the front again. When you run out of wire, twist the ends together at the back of the mesh dome. Repeat this step until the center is filled with a small burst of bead color.

4 Cut a 12-inch piece of the 26-gauge wire, then attach the seed beads around the outside of the center cluster. Keep attaching beads until the entire mesh dome is covered with small beads.

What You Need

Basic tool kit (page 17)

26-gauge wire

Mesh pin backing

Medium-sized beads

Seed beads in blue and red

What You Do

1 Cut a 12-inch piece of the 26-gauge wire. Detach the pin back from the circular mesh dome, then thread one of the wire ends through the mesh dome, going back to front. Slide one of the medium-sized beads onto the wire, then thread the wire back through the mesh dome, pulling it tight.

5 To fill out the firecracker formation and to fill in any gaps, add more small beads, leaving enough 26-gauge wire (about ¼ inch) between the mesh dome and each bead, so that you can twist the wire together two to three times. This will make the beads burst out from the pin. Then reattach the pin back to the mesh dome.

Fit-for-a-Queen Chandelier Necklace and Earrings

Bringing to mind the French court of the 18th century, this ornate chandelier design is a symbol of sophistication. Accented with green beads and freshwater pearls, these pieces sparkle with timeless elegance.

To make the necklace:
What You Need

Basic tool kit (page 17)

8 headpins (One should be 2 inches long.)

1 strand of freshwater pearls, 16 inches long, 2 mm diameter

20 clear crystal bicone beads, 4 mm diameter

1 oval purple bead, 18 x 13 mm (We used quartz beads.)

Chandelier finding

9 oval green beads, 8 mm (We used green aventurine beads.)

Tigertail wire

2 crimp beads

Clasp

Jump ring (optional)

Chain for necklace extender (optional)

What You Do

1 To make the chandelier pendant, slide a freshwater pearl onto the 2-inch headpin, then add a clear crystal bicone bead, the oval purple bead, a clear crystal bicone bead, and a pearl. Use the round-nose pliers to form a small loop in the end of the headpin, then slide the pin through the center bottom loop of the chandelier finding. Wrap the remaining wire two to three times between the loop and the pearl, then trim any excess wire.

2 Slide a freshwater pearl onto another headpin, then add a clear crystal bicone bead and another pearl. Make a loop in the end of the headpin with the round-nose pliers, and slide the pin through the loop adjacent to the beaded wire from step 1. Wrap the remaining wire two to three times between the loop and the pearl, then trim any excess wire. Repeat this step, then attach the headpin to the other side of the beaded wire from step 1.

3 Slide a freshwater pearl onto another headpin, then add a clear crystal bicone bead, an oval green bead, a clear crystal bicone bead, and another pearl. Make a loop in the headpin with the pliers, then slide the pin through the loop adjacent to one of the beaded wires from step 2. Wrap the remaining wire two to three times between the loop and the pearl, and trim any excess wire. Repeat this step until the bottom loops of the chandelier finding are all filled.

4 To make the pearl strand, cut a 21-inch piece of the tigertail wire, then thread 3½ inches of freshwater pearls onto the wire. Add a clear crystal bicone bead, an oval green bead, and a clear crystal bicone bead. Then thread another 3½ inches of pearls onto the strand, followed by a crystal bicone bead, an oval green bead, and another bicone bead. Add the beaded chandelier finding, followed by a bicone bead, a green bead, and another bicone bead on the opposite side of the stand. Then thread on 3½ inches of pearls, followed by a bicone bead, a green bead, and another bicone bead. Finish out the strand with another 3½ inches of pearls.

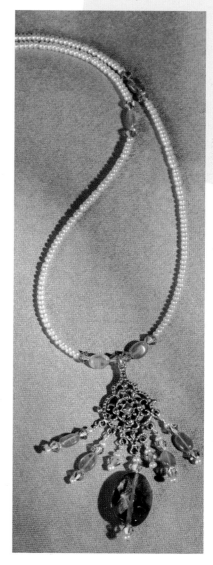

5 Add a crimp bead to each end of the strand, then take one end of the strand and thread it through the clasp's loop. Thread the wire back through the crimp bead and the first few pearls, and pull the end of the wire until the crimp bead butts up against the clasp. Then crimp the bead and trim away any excess wire. Repeat this step with the opposite end of the strand, using the jump ring or, if you decide to make the necklace extender below, the end link of the chain.

6 To make the necklace extender, cut a 2½-inch piece of the chain and follow step 5 to attach it to the necklace. Then slide a crystal bicone bead, a green bead, and a bicone bead onto a headpin. Form a loop in the end of the pin with the round-nose pliers, and slide the pin through the remaining end of the chain. Wrap any remaining wire around the pin between the bottom of the loop and the top of the bead using the needle-nose pliers. Trim any excess wire.

To make the earrings:

What You Need

Basic tool kit (page 17)

14 headpins (Two of them should be 2 inches long.)

28 freshwater pearls, 2 mm diameter

30 clear crystal bicone beads, 4 mm diameter

2 violet round beads, 6 mm diameter (We used amethyst beads.)

14 oval green beads, 8 mm diameter (We used green aventurine beads.)

2 chandelier findings

2 earring wires

What You Do

1 Slide a freshwater pearl onto one of the 2-inch headpins, then add beads in the following order: one clear crystal bicone bead, one violet bead, one clear crystal bicone bead, one oval green bead, one clear crystal bicone bead, and one freshwater pearl. Then use the round-nose pliers to make a small loop in the headpin. Slide this loop through the center bottom loop of one of the chandelier findings and wrap the remaining wire two to three times between the loop and the pearl. Trim any excess wire.

2 Slide a freshwater pearl onto a headpin (not the other 2-inch headpin), then add beads in the following order: one clear crystal bicone bead, one oval green bead, one clear crystal bicone bead, and one freshwater pearl. Then make a loop in the headpin with the pliers, and slide it through the loop adjacent to the beaded wire from step 1. Wrap

the remaining wire two to three times between the loop and the pearl, and trim any excess wire. Repeat this step five additional times until the bottom loops of the chandelier finding are all filled.

3 Use the pliers to open the bottom loop of an earring wire. Slip the earring wire through the top loop of the chandelier finding, then close it with the pliers. Repeat all of the steps to make the matching earring.

tip —•◦•—

Chandelier findings can have anywhere from two to 10 loops (or any number in between) for attaching beads. Adding just a few beads hearkens back to the Victorian era. Adding lots of beads will give the piece a bohemian feel. Add as many or as few beads as you like—it all depends on your personal vision, and on what era appeals to you.

Tidbit:
Earring styles are strongly affected by hairstyles. When enormous powdered wigs were worn by the French court in the 18th century, earrings such as these needed to be large and elaborate just to be seen. Conversely, earrings all but disappeared a century later when women wore their hair severely parted in the center and pulled to the back in a tight knot, completely obscuring the ears.

Playful Pearls and IoliteNecklace

Colorful pearls pair up with bright blue iolite beads for a fun, loose,

flapper-inspired necklace.

What You Need

Basic tool kit (page 17)

Tigertail wire

**94 crystal bicone beads,
4 mm diameter**

**47 dyed freshwater pearls
(can be irregularly shaped),
8 mm diameter**

**47 rectangular iolite beads,
8 x 4 mm**

Crimp bead

What You Do

1 Cut a 40-inch piece of the tigertail wire, then string on a crystal bead and a freshwater pearl. Add another crystal bead, then an iolite bead. Repeat this pattern 46 more times until the necklace is 36 inches long.

2 Slide a crimp bead onto one end of the wire, then thread the other end of the wire through the crimp bead, going in the opposite direction. Using the needle-nose pliers, crimp the bead. Trim away any excess wire.

Garnet and Citrine Earrings

Red simply never goes out of style. The classic color looks particularly elegant here,

combined with golden citrine beads and silver wire.

What You Need

Basic tool kit (page 17)

24-gauge wire

6 citrine briolette or teardrop-shaped beads, 6 mm

8 garnet beads, 6 x 4 mm

2 earring findings with multiple loops

2 earring wires

What You Do

1 Cut a 2½-inch piece of the 24-gauge wire, then slide one end through the top of one of the citrine beads, making sure a ½-inch length of the wire emerges from the other side. Wrap this ½-inch length two to three times around the other part of the wire at the top of the bead, and trim any excess wire from this end.

2 Slide a garnet bead onto the remaining wire, which should be sticking straight up from the citrine bead. Use the round-nose pliers to form a loop in the wire, then slide this loop through a loop at the bottom of one of the earring findings. Wrap the remaining wire two to three times between the loop and the garnet bead, and trim any excess wire.

3 Repeat steps 1 and 2 two more times, or as many times as you need to fill out the bottom loops of the earring finding.

4 Cut a 2-inch piece of the 24-gauge wire, make a loop in one end using the round-nose pliers, and slip the loop around the loop at the top of the earring finding. Wrap the wire two to three times at the base of the loop, and add a garnet bead. Then make a loop in the opposite end of the wire and slip it through the bottom loop of one of the earring wires. Wrap the wire two to three times between the loop and the garnet bead, and trim any excess wire. Repeat all of the steps to make the other earring.

Roaring Twenties Tasseled Necklace

Celebrate the spirit of the Roaring Twenties with this

stylish concoction of beads.

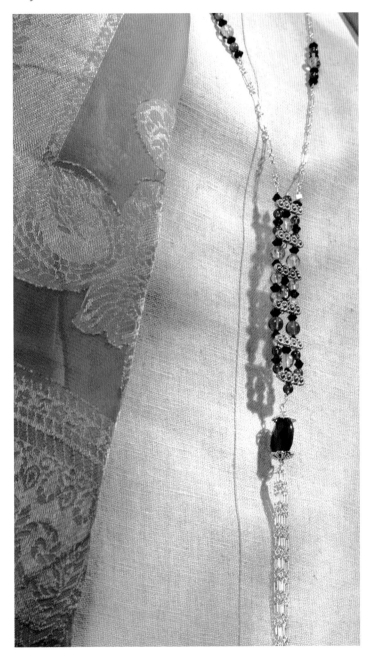

What You Need

Basic tool kit (page 17)

Tigertail wire

18 crimp beads

6 marcasite spacer beads, each with 3 holes, 15 mm diameter

18 round amethyst beads, 4 mm diameter

54 red crystal bicone beads, 4 mm diameter

12 round peridot beads, 4 mm diameter

8 faceted pale green crystal beads, 6 mm diameter

Sterling silver chain

24-gauge wire

2 bead caps, 10 mm diameter

1 faceted oval red candy quartz bead, 18 x 12 mm

7 round amethyst beads, 6 mm diameter

What You Do

1 Cut a 7-inch piece of the tigertail wire, slide a crimp bead onto the wire, then slip one end of the strand through the side hole in one of the marcasite spacer beads. Thread ½ inch of the wire back through the crimp bead, and pull the long end of the wire tight so that the crimp bead butts up against the spacer bead's loop. Crimp the bead, and trim away any excess from the wire's short end.

2 Slide a 4 mm round amethyst bead, a red bicone bead, and another 4 mm amethyst bead onto the tigertail wire. Thread another marcasite spacer bead onto the wire, then add a red bicone bead, a 6 mm round amethyst bead, and another red bicone bead. String on another spacer bead, followed by a round peridot bead, a red bicone bead, and another peridot bead. Then string on a spacer bead, a red bicone bead, a pale green crystal bead, and a red bicone bead. Add another spacer bead, followed by a 4 mm round amethyst bead, a red bicone bead, and another 4 mm amethyst bead. Slide on one more spacer bead, a 4 mm round amethyst bead, and then a crimp bead.

3 Cut a 2¼-inch length of the silver chain, then slide the free end of the tigertail wire through one of the end links of the chain. Repeat the crimping process in step 1 to attach the two pieces. Then repeat steps 2 and 3 on the other side of the marcasite spacer beads.

4 Cut a 2-inch piece of the 24-gauge wire, grasp the wire with the round-nose pliers ½ inch from the end, and make a small loop. Then wrap the wire end around the base of the loop two to three times. Trim any excess wire.

5 Thread a 4 mm round amethyst bead onto the 24-gauge wire, then slide the wire through the center hole of the last marcasite spacer bead. Add a red bicone bead, a pale green crystal bead, and another red bicone bead. Slip the wire through the center hole of the next spacer bead, grip the wire on the other side of the spacer bead with the pliers, and form another loop. Wrap the remaining wire two to three times between the loop and the spacer bead, then trim any excess

wire. Repeat steps 1 through 5 on the other side and on the bottom of the spacer beads.

6 Cut ten 3¼-inch pieces of the silver chain and a 2-inch piece of the 24-gauge wire. Form a loop in one end of the wire using the round-nose pliers, then slide an end loop from each length of the chain onto this loop, and wrap the wire two to three times above the loop to secure it. Trim any excess wire.

7 Slide a bead cap onto the wire, add the oval red candy quartz bead, then the other bead cap. Form a loop in the end of the wire, and slide it through the bottom loop from the end of step 5. Wrap the remaining wire two to three times between the loop and the bead cap to secure the pendant, then trim any excess wire.

8 Cut a 3-inch piece of the tigertail wire. Slide a crimp bead onto both ends of the wire. Then thread a red bicone bead onto the wire, followed by a 4 mm round amethyst bead, a red bicone bead, a pale green crystal bead, a red bicone, a 4 mm amethyst bead, and a red bicone bead.

9 Add crimp beads to both ends of the wire, then take one end of the wire and thread it through the remaining end loop of the silver chain length from step 3. Thread the wire back through the crimp bead and the first red bead. Pull the end of the wire until the crimp bead butts up against the end loop, then crimp the bead. Trim any excess wire.

10 Cut a 2¼-inch length of the chain, and crimp the remaining end of the beaded tigertail wire to an end loop of the chain. Make sure to pull the wire until it's tight, so that no gaps remain between the beads. Repeat steps 8 through 10 on the other side.

11 Cut a 3-inch piece of the tigertail wire, then string a red bicone bead, a round peridot bead, a red bicone bead, a 6 mm round amethyst bead, a red bicone bead, a peridot bead, and another red bicone bead onto the wire. Repeat steps 9 and 10. Then repeat step 11 in its entirety on the other side.

12 Repeat steps 8 through 11 so that you have a total of eight beaded wires. Attach the last two beaded wires to opposite ends of the same chain length.

tip —◆●◆—

If you like, you can use a chain with tiny loops for the pieces that dangle from the pendant, then switch to a chain with larger loops for the body of the necklace. The smaller loops will keep your pendant from appearing too bulky and overwhelming the rest of the piece.

Lassoed Pearls

You'll be dripping with pearls—and elegance—when you wear this lariat necklace. Simply slip all of the strands through the beaded wire hoop, then let the pearls drape in front, in back, or to the side—it's your choice!

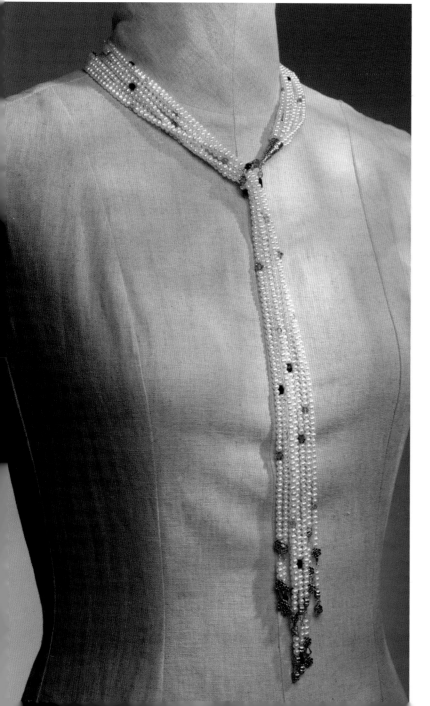

What You Need

Basic tool kit (page 17)

Silver flower beads

7 headpins, each at least 2 inches long

Crystal beads in a variety of colors, 4 mm and 6 mm diameter

15 strands of freshwater pearls, each 16 inches long, 4 mm diameter

Tigertail wire

14 crimp beads

22-gauge wire

Silver cone, 1 inch long

Wire earring hoop with loop in one end, 1 inch diameter

What You Do

1 String a silver flower bead onto one of the headpins, then add a crystal bead, another silver flower bead, and three freshwater pearls. Use the round-nose pliers to grasp the headpin, and form a loop about ½ inch from the end. Wrap the remaining wire two to three times between the loop and the first pearl, then trim away any excess wire. Repeat this step six additional times.

2 Cut a 32-inch piece of the tigertail wire, and add a crimp bead to one end. Thread the wire end through the loop of one of the headpins, then back through the crimp bead again. Use the needle-nose pliers to crush the crimp bead, then trim away any excess wire.

3 Thread a silver floral bead onto the tigertail wire, then add 1 inch of pearls. Follow with a crystal bead, then 5 inches of pearls. Continue adding one crystal bead and 5 inches of pearls until you have a string that's 28 inches long.

4 Repeat step 3 again. Then repeat it two more times, but instead of using 1 inch of pearls to begin the strand, add 2 inches of pearls after the silver flower bead. Repeat step 3 two more times, adding 3 inches of pearls after the silver flower bead each time. Then repeat the step, this time adding 4 inches of pearls at the beginning. Repeat the step a final time with 5 inches of pearls at the beginning, so that you have a total of eight strands. Add crimp beads to both ends of each strand.

5 Cut a 2½-inch piece of the 22-gauge wire, then use the round-nose pliers to form a loop in the wire large enough to hold four pearl strands. Wrap the tail of the 22-gauge wire two to three times around the base of the loop to secure it. Take the end of one pearl strand and thread it through the wire loop, then back through the crimp bead on the strand. Pull the pearl strand tight so that no gaps remain between the beads, then crush the crimp bead with the needle-nose pliers,

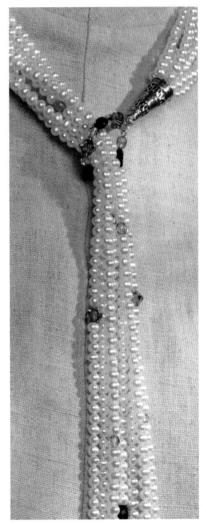

and trim away any excess wire. Add three more pearl strands in the same fashion, then repeat the entire step with the remaining four strands.

6 Thread both wires from step 5 through the wide end of the silver cone so that the opposite ends of the wires protrude from the tip of the cone. Then gather the two wires together and make a single loop with both of them, using the round-nose pliers.

7 String crystal beads onto the earring hoop. Use the round-nose pliers to form a loop in the straight end. Then hook the two loops together and secure them with the needle-nose pliers. Slide the double-wire loop emerging from the silver cone over and around the hooked loops of the wire hoop. Wrap the doubled wire two to three times between the loop and the cone tip, and trim any excess wire (see figure 1).

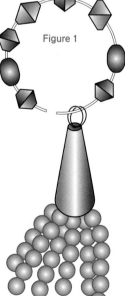

Figure 1

tip

For a variation on this design, try using small crystal beads or semi-precious stones instead of pearls.

119

Silver Cabbage Rose Necklace

Elegant

What's more Victorian than a cabbage rose? Here, eye-catching carnelian teardrops complement the sterling silver bloom.

What You Need

Basic tool kit (page 17)

Tigertail wire

112 teardrop beads, 10 x 4 mm

Cabbage rose pendant,
45 to 60 mm diameter

2 crimp beads

Jump ring

Clasp

What You Do

1 Cut a 20-inch piece of the tigertail wire, then string 56 teardrop beads (about 8 inches) onto the wire, and add the cabbage rose pendant. (The pendant we used is 55 mm in diameter.) Then string 56 more teardrop beads onto the other side of the pendant.

2 String a crimp bead onto each end of the necklace. Thread the jump ring onto one end of the strand, then wind the wire around and back through the crimp bead. Pull the end of the wire until the crimp bead butts up against the jump ring, then crimp the bead using the needle-nose pliers. Trim away any excess wire with the scissors.

3 Repeat step 2 on the other end of the strand with the clasp, making sure the wire is pulled tightly enough before crimping so that no gaps remain between the beads.

tip ——•••——

A pendant as dramatic as this cabbage rose is best accompanied by beads that don't steal center stage. Small teardrop beads like the ones used here work well because they add color and texture without detracting from the impact of the flower.

When stringing a large number of teardrop beads together, it's easy to leave gaps between them. Remember to pull the wire tight before securing the strand with a crimp bead.

121

About the Authors

Marty Stevens-Heebner and Christine Calla both design jewelry for Half the Sky (www.half-the-sky.com). Marty's work has been featured in *A Closet Full of Shoes: Simple Ways to Make Them Chic* (Sterling/Chapelle, 2006) as well as in magazines such as *Belle Armoire* and *Altered Couture*. She's also appeared on HGTV and the DIY network. In addition to being an accomplished designer, Christine is the mother of three—she includes her husband in that tally. You can contact the authors at Marty@half-the-sky.com or Christine@half-the-sky.com.

Acknowledgments

Our deepest gratitude goes to everyone at Lark Books for their help and support during the writing of this book—especially Paige Gilchrist, our amazing editor Kathy Sheldon, and Julie Hale. It's thanks to the keen eyes of art director Susan McBride and photographer Keith Wright that the projects pop off these pages. We're grateful to Marcia Parisi for getting us started, and we never could have kept things organized amid the chaos of creating this book were it not for Nicole Martinez and Jeanne Lusignan. Finally, we thank Tammy Honaman and Fire Mountain Gems for supplying us with the beautiful gemstones and findings that enliven the jewelry in our projects.

Fire Mountain Gems
One Fire Mountain Way
Grants Pass, OR 97526
(800) 355-2137
www.FireMountainGems.com

Glossary

The following is a list of terms used in this book as well as ones you may encounter when purchasing supplies for your vintage jewelry projects.

Bail
A metal loop used to attach a pendant to a necklace.

Bezel
A grooved ring or rim holding a bead, watch crystal, gem, etc., in its setting.

Bi
Small disks used as ceremonial pieces in ancient China, bi can be made of jade or other stones.

Bicone
A bead shaped like two stacked cones with their widest parts joined in the middle and the points on either end.

Briolette
A bead with a teardrop shape. It can have a faceted or unfaceted surface.

Cabochon
An undrilled and unfaceted bead with a domed surface.

Carat
When spelled in this manner, the term usually refers to the weight of a gemstone. See also "karat."

Carnelian
A form of quartz, this translucent gemstone ranges in color from a clear orange red to an opaque dark orange brown.

Crimp Bead
Crimp beads resemble small metal beads or tubes and are used to connect a clasp or other connector to beading wire.

Drop Bead
Any bead with a hole through the top instead of through the middle.

Extender
A piece of chain used to lengthen beaded jewelry.

Filigree
A very elaborate form of jewelry metalwork that features lacy scrolls and delicate spirals made of extremely fine silver, gold, or other precious metal wire.

Finding
The general term for jewelry-making components (usually made of metal) that are used to hold beads or string elements together. Examples include earring hooks, jump rings, and clasps.

Fine Silver
An alloy made of 99.9 percent pure silver.

Gauge
A standard series of sizes indicating the thickness or diameter of wire. The higher the gauge, the thinner the wire. For example, 24-gauge wire is thinner than 18-gauge wire.

Gold-Filled or Gold Overlay
Wire that has been subjected to heat and pressure in order to add a layer of gold to a base of inexpensive base metal.

Gold- or Silver-Plated
Wire or metal that has been coated via an electro-chemical process with a very thin layer of either 24-karat gold or fine silver.

Karat
A number between one and 24 that indicates the level of pure gold in a sample of gold wire. Pure gold is called 24 karat because 24 parts out of 24 are gold, whereas 18 karat indicates that only 18 out of 24 parts are gold, meaning 75 percent of that sample is pure and the remaining 25 percent is made up of metals other than gold. Also abbreviated "kt" and sometimes spelled "carat."

Lavaliere

An elaborately jeweled ornamental pendant worn on a chain around the neck.

Mandrel

A long cylindrical shape, usually made from wood or steel, that is used to shape and curve metalwork. It is most often used for making rings.

Marcasite

The mineral itself is a crystallized form of iron pyrite, but the term also refers to any piece of metalwork or jewelry that features the mineral as part of its ornamentation. It was especially popular during the 18th century.

Rondele

A popular bead shape, this thick disk has either flat or pointed sides (like a somewhat flattened bicone bead) with a hole through the middle. Rondeles can be faceted or unfaceted.

Rutilated Quartz

Quartz containing deposits of rutile, a mineral composed mainly of titanium dioxide, which can give off a shiny golden appearance inside the quartz.

Semi-Precious

A variety of stones that are valued for their beauty and color—including amethysts, garnets, and citrines—but are not as costly as those deemed "precious," such as diamonds, rubies, and sapphires.

Serrated Pliers

Pliers that have grooves or teeth to provide a good, firm grip. Care must be taken when using serrated pliers because these grooves can mar beading wire.

Sterling Silver

A common and easy-to-work alloy of silver made of 92.5 percent pure silver and 7.5 percent copper. It often bears the stamp ".925."

Tigertail Wire

An excellent beading wire comprised of ultra-thin, braided stainless steel cables covered with nylon. It drapes a bit more rigidly than thread and is a must for heavier necklaces.

Vermeil

Metal, such as silver or bronze that has been gilded with a fine layer of gold.

Metric Conversion Table

Inches	Centimeters	Inches	Centimeters
1/8	3 mm	12	30
1/4	6 mm	13	32.5
3/8	9 mm	14	35
1/2	1.3	15	37.5
5/8	1.6	16	40
3/4	1.9	17	42.5
7/8	2.2	18	45
1	2.5	19	47.5
1 1/4	3.1	20	50
1 1/2	3.8	21	52.5
1 3/4	4.4	22	55
2	5	23	57.5
2 1/2	6.25	24	60
3	7.5	25	62.5
3 1/2	8.8	26	65
4	10	27	67.5
4 1/2	11.3	28	70
5	12.5	29	72.5
5 1/2	13.8	30	75
6	15	31	77.5
7	17.5	32	80
8	20	33	82.5
9	22.5	34	85
10	25	35	87.5
11	27.5	36	90

Index

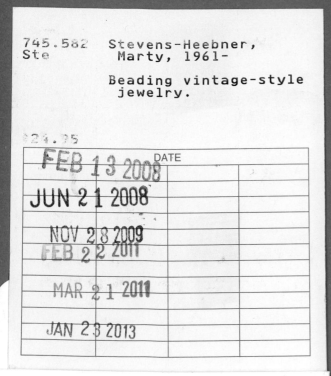